Children and Literature

Edited by
Shubha Tiwari

ATLANTIC®
PUBLISHERS & DISTRIBUTORS

Published by

ATLANTIC®

PUBLISHERS & DISTRIBUTORS

B-2, Vishal Enclave, Opp. Rajouri Garden,
New Delhi-110027
Phones : 25413460, 25429987, 25466842

Sales Office
7/22, Ansari Road, Darya Ganj,
New Delhi-110002
Phones : 23273880, 23275880, 23280451
Fax : 91-11-23285873
web : www.atlanticbooks.com
e-mail : info@atlanticbooks.com

ISBN 81-269-0583-2

Printed in India
at Nice Printing Press, Delhi

Preface

Once there was a woman who could never be free from domestic chores. Her six years old son used to feel neglected. Often he used to coax his mother to take him out to some fair or show. On a festive occasion the mother decided to take the child to a fair. Promptly she completed her daily chores, dressed herself and the child and the duo went to the fair. The woman felt so happy. Colourful balloons, fancy kites, music, sight of delicious eatables, stalls of jewels and clothes made her run around and fill her eyes with shining sights. But to her utter dismay, her son who was walking beside her, kept crying, and complaining. He said that he wanted to go home. The woman got irritated. She slapped her son and bent down to pick him up in her lap. As she bent down to pick the child, she got glimpse of the view from the child's height. What she saw was appalling. All around, there were peels, wrappers and spit. Then she understood the difference between her view and that of the child. She realized the importance of seeing things from the point of view of the child.

Our world is amazingly and completely adult-centred. The environment, education, games, books, advertisements and even comics, movies and teleserials are out and out adult-centred. Adults decide what children should consume intellectually or otherwise. There have been very rare attempts to see things from the eyes of children. It is a very tedious task. It is just like seeing the world for the first time. Our worldly coating is so strong that it becomes impossible for the most of us to see things from the eyes of the children. This goal has probably been achieved partially in the present anthology. Views on children's literature as well as child characters in literature have been studied.

We, the teacher-critics, enjoy in writing about man-woman relationship, themes of alienation, diaspora, rootlessness, and related areas of absurdism and nihilism. These are fashionable topics. The adventurous tread on zones like feminism, post-colonialism etc. Here also the forum, the person, and the intricacy of the topic decide the way a piece is going to be received. If I am not totally wrong, there seems to be pervading eliticism in our field.

To think of those who cannot effectively voice their concerns can be safely taken as a parameter of development of civilization. Development of sensitivity towards categories other than one's own is an appealing and noble idea. It is in this spirit, the present volume has been prepared.

There is quite a lot of mental chaos over childhood-adulthood phenomena. Growing up is unduly, undeservedly stressed. Every child is exasperatingly told, 'Grow up! When will you grow up!' whereas the ideal situation would be where every adult is encouraged to be a child, at least in some measures. The whole problem is that all of us are so hopelessly grown up. We are ever so scared of making a child-like mistake, of behaving like a child, of not being grown up.

The common concept of growing up is also interesting. Growing up is about not being deceived by others or even better, deceiving others. It is about making lots of money, no matter which means are employed to gain that money. It is about being successful, at any rate. Mario Puzo tells in *The God-father*, 'Ditch the world before it ditches you.' A grown-up person is expected to one's own trumpet all the time. S/he should subtly manage rewards, awards, honours, settle scores, manipulate processes and conspire against enemies. Indulged in all this murky business, a grown-up person looks innocent, innocuous, pleasant and trustworthy. Growing up also means never trusting anyone, always doubting, always smelling a plot. An important characteristic of full-grown person is her/his knack at the art of flattery. In short, a mature person is nothing less than sugar coated poison, a deadly flower, a cup of murdering nectar.

To rectify this imbalance in our perception, discussion on children's literature, and children in literature is required. In the present anthology, critics have discussed childhood phenomenon in its various dimensions and levels.

The first paper by Basavraj Naikar is a wonderful account of wonders of childhood. The boy named Rishi has a unique experience of growing up in colonial India. The write-up catches the spirit of freedom and newness in childhood. The second paper by Mary Conde discusses an entirely different area of adolescence as it is elaborated in Tsitsi Dangarembga's *Nervous Conditions*. The special contribution of the paper is that it discusses 'food' as a major symbol of adolescent thinking as it is portrayed in the novel. Next comes my own paper where I have tried to establish that Gandhi was sober and sublime because he completely missed the phenomenon called childhood. His missed childhood played a significant role in shaping his thinking, his dutiful acceptance of social responsibilities. The next paper by B. Parvathy celebrates the much celebrated version of carefree model of Indian childhood, namely R.K. Narayan's Swamy. Then a paper on Mahasweta Devi's *Bayen* by Madhu Singh delineates the complexities of a complicated case of an adolescent. Alka Saxena touches very emotional aspect of depiction of childhood by Indian women. The story actually belongs to almost every Indian girl as she is held inferior to her brother/s; she is admonished at childish behaviour; and she is almost never pampered. In the same tone, the next paper discusses the touching figure of girl child in Indian fiction in English. Going on a larger perspective, Purnima Mehta discusses pre-adolescence in modern English fiction. *Panchtantra* and *Aesop's Fables* have been compared by Sadhana Agrawal. Marina Goglio discusses the idea of threat to innocence by its contact with maturity with special reference to three Indian English novels. The phenomenon of Harry Potter, the role of fiction in growing up and evolution of clever writing in the field of children's literature have been dealt by Esterino Adami. Shubha Dwivedi discusses a landmark novel in child psychology, *Apka Bunty*. A unique idea of childhood in the poetry of Robert Frost has been portrayed by Awadhesh K. Mishra. The next paper by Neha Nigam may look a little out of place but it is actually not so. The paper describes the problems of childhood purely in psychological terms. The last paper of the anthology compares and contrasts the childhood of two towering personalities of 20th century, namely M.K. Gandhi and Adolf Hitler. Kiran Shukla, in this paper, tries to see how childhood shaped this saintly man called Gandhi and how it shaped one of the cruelest human beings of all times, Hitler.

It is hoped that the present anthology will prove immensely informative and interesting not only to the students and teachers of English literature but also to the general readers interested in child psychology.

My genuine thanks are due to Dr. K.R. Gupta, Chairman, Atlantic Publishers and Distributors for publishing this offstage idea called *Children and Literature*.

SHUBHA TIWARI

Contents

1

Childhood Experience in *Rishi*

Basavaraj Naikar

The number of novels dealing with childhood experience is very limited in world literature when compared to those dealing with adult experience. The Anglo-Indian fiction is no exception to this. *Rishi* by Taya Zinkin belongs to the rare species of fiction dealing with the protagonist's experience of childhood. But a special thing to be remembered is that it is not part of children's literature nor is it an autobiographical picture of the narrator's childhood. On the contrary, it is a novel written by a mature author about the experiences of a child through the technique of omniscient narration.

The title of the novel *Rishi* is very misleading in that it gives an impression of the ascetic life that might have been depicted in it. But when one opens and reads through it, one finds oneself in the midst of childhood experiences of a British boy born in India just before the expiry of the colonial rule in the subcontinent. It deals with the colourful experiences of the British boy from his birth to his school-going age during which period he is made to stay in India. The novelist Taya Zinkin offers very beautiful insights into child psychology not only by probing the mind of a child, but by depicting the child mind against the background of bicultural encounter between Britain and India.

The main action of the novel happens just before the independence of India around 1946 when the British were about to leave the colonized country. The child protagonist is born to the British parents, *i.e.* Sally and Peter Clarence who have been living in India. Peter Clarence has been a member of Indian Civil Service of the British Administration of India. He and his wife Sally have been living in a spacious house in New Delhi.

The colourful encounter between Britain and India was paradoxically marked by a love-hate relationship. Though politically they hated each other, emotionally they had cordial relationship with each other. But in the present novel the cordial relationship between the British and the Indians is foregrounded whereas the political hatred between the two is relegated to the background.

It is on account of the emotional attachment for India and Indian culture that Sally and Peter Clarence decide to christen their child as 'Rishi,' which has multiple cultural connotations. India, which is known as a land of *rishis* easily suggests the spiritual achievements of saints and *yogis* of the land. The Clarence couple naming their child as 'Rishi' is obviously, indicative of their attachment, love and admiration for India and her culture. It also shows their wishful desire that their son should be another *rishi* or visionary. It is this cordial relationship with the colonized country that softens their political stance for the same.

Rishi is thus a British boy bearing an Indian, especially Hindu name. He is made by the circumstances of his life to lead an amphibian life between two cultures, *i.e.* British and Indian. It is against this background that he encounters the world around him through his growing consciousness. The novelist tries to delineate the child's observation of and reaction to the world. His perception of the world is partly natural and partly colonial and together it provides a very interesting experience for us. Through the depiction of the child's reaction to the environment—including things, beings and events, the novelist reveals the working of a child's mind and provides good material for the application of child psychology.

Rishi is born in a hospital at Delhi in 1946 and is affectionately watched by the servants like old Dias and Abdul and even by the dog called 'Pish'. Rishi, the newborn baby is not conscious of anything around him. But he slowly develops the consciousness of the world after a lapse of one year after his birth. It is only then that he learns the pronunciation of Pish and develops a sort of friendship with it. But by then India achieves independence on 15th August 1947, which is accompanied by communal violence among Hindus and Muslims involving mutual stabbing and burning etc. The one-year old child Rishi is, therefore, sent to England by his mother so that he would be taken care of by his grandmother there. Rishi returns to India along with his parents two years after independence and stays in Bombay and later moves to the city of Calcutta.

Like most children, Rishi has a special liking for animals. That is the reason why he used to be friendly with the dog Pish and observe its pranks and movements with great curiosity and fellow feeling. He feels deeply saddened when the dog is gifted away to a Frenchman called Dupont by his parents before their departure to England. On his fourth birthday Sally presents him a guinea pig as a gift. Rishi enjoys playing with it. Similarly Rishi wants to observe the monkeys with great curiosity and admiration not realizing how troublesome they can be. Once the garden in front of Rishi's house is crowded with a large group of monkeys. A baby monkey picks up a burning cigarette-end and puts it into its mouth and screeches because of the pain of being burnt. Consequently some forty or so monkeys march on the lawn to scare Sally. But Sally lifts up Rishi and rushes into the house and bangs the door. Rishi, in spite of his general admiration for monkeys, asks his mother as to why his father should not shoot them down. His mother answers him in the negative and explains the Indian, especially Hindu cultural background according to which 'monkeys are sacred in India and nobody can hurt them' (52).

Rishi takes a special interest in the lion-cub, which is gifted by the Government of Saurastra to Sally. When Sally brings it home in a wooden cage, Rishi grows ecstatic about it. But when the lion-cub disturbs the peace of the family and the neighbourhood, Rishi is also scared by it. He likes the animal so much that he names it as 'Asha' after his own little girl friend. One day when a party is going on, Rishi's friend Fardoon hits the lion-cub with a brick and is bitten by it on his knee. Consequently the whole party is disturbed. Finally Sally realizes her folly and sends the animal to the London zoo. Rishi enjoys watching the crows on the sea-side trees although they pose a problem to the elders. When he is taken by His Highness Shivaji to the private zoo at Porbandar, he enjoys watching the black bucks, hyena and tiger-cubs.

Like most children, Rishi enjoys watching the world around him with extraordinary curiosity and enriching his knowledge of life. The cultural contrast between England and India adds to his curiosity. He goes to Chowpatti along with his parents and friends to watch Ganapati Puja and the immersion of the idol into water. They hire a fisherman who takes them in a boat to enable them to watch the *puja*. Rishi and other children obviously enjoy the sight whole-heartedly. Similarly, Rishi enjoys the Durga Puja and the immersion of the idol in Hoogly River when he and his friends are taken to the spot by Uncle Chattopadhyaya. He tries to understand the symbolic significance of the ritual explained by Chattopadhyaya.

The child mind is known for its innocence, which can be comic, hurting and embarrassing in different situations. Rishi exhibits a good deal of such innocence in his encounter with the people in India. For example, Mr. Khandelawalla has lost his son Farouk almost of Rishi's age. The doctors opine that Farouk must have died of cerebral malaria. The Peters feel very sorry for Khandelawalla and therefore never refer to children or Farouk in his presence. They ask Rishi also not to be seen by Khandelawalla lest the latter should be reminded of his lost son. But in spite of the parental warning, Rishi asks Mr. Khandelawalla about Farouk's death, not knowing how much agony that reminder would cause to the bereaved father.

A child's mind is generally very rich in imagination and therefore builds up exaggerated picture of things and beings; but it is rather disappointed when reality falls short of ideals imaginatively conceived. For example, when the Peters plan to go to Ponderbur where they are likely to meet the Maharajah Shivaji, Rishi's mind becomes alert and conceives of a grand and very impressive regal personality of the Maharajah. But he feels rather disappointed to see the unregal appearance of the Maharajah who is clad in blue jeans. Similarly, when Rishi is taken to the residential quarter of a forest officer called Bahadur Singh, he imagines a glorious picture of the 'thunder box' referred to by people there. But later he is disappointed to know that it is only a commode.

Rishi, like all children, wants to extend the realm of his experience by learning new habits, especially the ones belonging not to the British but to the Indian culture, which is inclusive of Hindu and Muslim ones. His mother Sally does not like him to learn the alien habits, but Rishi, innocent as he is, is very eager to learn them not only for the pleasure of it, but for achieving close companionship with his friends. His innocent mind, which tries to see the unity of humanity, does not discriminate between the so-called superior culture and the inferior one or between the colonizer and the colonized. Rishi, for example, has developed a liking for typically Indian food items like a *chappatis*, *chana* and chillies. The servants in Clarence's house know that such habits are not approved by the British parents. One day Hari confidentially advises Abdul not to spoil Rishi with Indian food and eatable like *chappatis* and chillies lest his parents should dislike it. But Abdul does not have the heart to displease Rishi whenever the latter requests the former for *chappatis* and chillies. When Rishi goes to Bahadur Singh's house along with his parents, he faces the problem of cultural difference. When he has to have his food with Radha, eldest daughter of Bahadur Singh, he cannot identify the food items like *poori* and curds etc. He tries to imitate little Radha by eating with his fingers but miserably fails to do so. Radha, therefore, arranges to get a spoon for him. Rishi feels shy of not being able to eat with his fingers. He likes the curd immensely as it tastes like yogurt. A little later he learns how to eat with his fingers and drink water without touching the rim of the glass. Similarly, he wants to extend the frontiers of his experience by tasting new drinks. When Rishi's host Bahadur Singh asks him if he would taste *nira*, he does not know its meaning, but learns its meaning and wants to taste it. Bahadur Singh, therefore, orders the *mali* to climb up the palmyra tree and get *nira* in an earthen pot. Rishi, thus, tastes *nira* and finds it better than cider as it is sweeter than the latter.

Rishi feels so much attracted to the Oriental culture that he wants to practice some of the Hindu rites, but alas! he cannot do so as he is not born as a Hindu. One day Sally being a journalist and a personal friend of Sardar Vallabhbhai Patel attends the funeral of the great leader and watches the public burning of his body on the pyre. She does not wish to describe that scene to Rishi. But when he hears the description of the same from Hari, he feels sorry for not being a Hindu to light the funeral pyre of his father. Here the childlike habit of imitation is intensified by the colonial encounter and bicultural or even multicultural situation. Rishi has heard from his mother how the Parsis throw their dead on the Tower of Silence. Likewise he has heard about the Hindu belief in the transmigration of soul. But his childlike mind makes him believe not in the philosophical or symbolic truth of such beliefs and practices, but in the empirical or literal veracity of the same. He, for example, wants to experiment with funerals. He has a toy monkey (called Coco brought from England) with which he wants to experiment the funeral practices of different cultures. First he tries the Muslim practice. He, with his friends, wraps the toy-monkey in a towel and buries it under the nursery carpet. Then he tries the Parsi method by keeping the toy-monkey on the windowsill and waits for crows to come as vultures to devour the dead body of the monkey. But the crows refuse to do so. Then Rishi tries the Hindu practice by keeping the toy-monkey on a few bit of twigs and burns it. He waits to watch if the soul of the monkey leaves the body. But Abdul and Han get the smell and rush there to extinguish the fire.

On another occasion Rishi is presented a guinea pig as a gift by Sally. He likes it immensely and calls it Babar. He has heard about the Hindu belief in reincarnation. But being a child, he mistakes the philosophical truth for pragmatic truth. He, therefore, wants to kill the pig for fun just to see if the pig would be reborn as a Brahmin. He does not listen to Abdul's warning against it. Sally is really shocked by Rishi's experimentation with reincarnation and therefore gives away the pig to a friend of hers.

Being a child Rishi does not discriminate between native British culture and Indian (i.e. Hindu or Muslim) cultures. Sometimes he exhibits calf-love when he thinks that he is in love with Nisha, wife of Bahadur Singh. After a couple of days Rishi goes out with his father Peter and embarrasses him by asking him as to why he did not marry Nisha. Further he opines that his mummy, *i.e.* Sally is fat and old whereas Nisha is young, slim and beautiful. Although embarrassed by Rishi's absurd questions, Peter tries to convince him by saying that he has married Sally according to his choice.

Though a British boy born in India, Rishi has come to know a few details of Muslim and Hindu cultures. He, for example, knows that a Muslim can legally marry up to four times. He, therefore, tells Abdul one day that he wants to have two wives, one like Nisha with black eyes and black hair and another with blue eyes. This attitude of Rishi speaks of his desire to see the unity of life and his ignorance of the inalienability of cultural behaviour. Abdul, the servant tells him that he cannot do so legally. Then Rishi says that he would become a Mussalman so that he can get up to four wives. But Abdul convinces him that having one wife is better than two or many wives, as it would be very difficult to lead a happy life.

Rishi is deeply interested in human bondage. He is so much attached to Abdul that he persuades the latter not to go to Nasirabad but to stay in Bombay with them. But Abdul is firm about his decision because of his 'ijjat'. Tears trickle in his eyes. Rishi is sensible enough to understand Abdul's feelings and does not want to trouble him. Abdul tells Rishi that he would like to open a bicycle shop at his native place. One month after Abdul's departure, a merchant friend of Abdul with red beard comes and enquires after Rishi's well being and hands over Abdul's gifts and takes back Rishi's gift. After six months Rishi gets a letter from Abdul advising him to take care of his health. Thus both the boys, Rishi and Abdul maintain a cordial relationship with each other, uncontaminated by communal, racial or national prejudices.

Rishi, like any typical boy, wants to please and surprise his mother by indulging in some adventures thereby proving his competence. One day he goes to the beach along with his mother. When Sally starts talking to Uma, Rishi stealthily goes to a palm tree and climbs it. He thinks that he is alone on the tree and feels proud of himself. But he is surprised to know that another boy Balwant Rao Yashvant Rao Chavan has already climbed the same tree much above Rishi. This simple event shows the boys' ambition to achieve something in life and the simultaneous realization of the difficulties involved in it in the midst of competition. In Freudian terms Rishi's desire to climb the tree symbolizes his ambition to rise high in life. When Chavan jumps to the ground, Rishi also climbs down the palm tree. His mother Sally introduces Rishi to Chavan and his sister Uma. Rishi feels rather disappointed to know that he does not have a long name like Balwant Rao and wishes to have one like that. 'Rishi felt touched, and at the same time very annoyed at the thought that he had only a short silly name like Rishi, and that there was no special name by which he could tell his friends to call him. He decided immediately that he would give his children very long and important names' (148). Rishi's desire to have such a long name is suggestive of the boyish desire to imitate the other people without knowing the practical and cultural difficulties involved in it.

Rishi, Balwant Rao and Uma grow into thick friends, although their parents come from different backgrounds. For example, Balwant Rao and Uma's mother Sushila Chavan teaches biology in Bombay University whereas the father Krishna Chavan has been a companion of Mahatma Gandhi. Balwant Rao is born on the Independence Day of India. Rishi and Balwant Rao dig canals and high dams for sport. Rishi is a supporter of big projects like Bhakra Dam whereas Balwant Rao is a supporter of small projects. 'Rishi was a supporter of the big projects, like the Bhakra Dam, the highest dam in the world, which Sally had described to him after a visit. But Babu was in favour, like his father, of small-scale irrigation' (151). The ideas of the two boys suggest their natures and priorities. Whereas Rishi is over ambitious, Babu happens to be contented. Whereas Rishi is idealistic and farsighted, Babu happens to be practical and shortsighted. When the two boys quarrel with each other on account of their ideological differences, Rishi's mother convinces him that what India needs is both the big and the small projects. 'But darling, you are both right. India needs the Bhakra Dam, but it also needs a well in every village. For how are people to live without water?' (152). Convinced by the mother's answer and guided by her, Rishi renews his friendship with Babu (or Balwant Rao). Rishi's behaviour illustrates the juvenile psychology in that the boys may quarrel with each other as quickly as they can be reconciled to each other. Thus quarrelling and chumming up go on alternating in juvenile life which is marked by the absence of deep seated malice or hatred.

The juvenile friendship between Rishi and Balwant Rao is characterized by a quest for the knowledge of alien cultures and desire to overcome the cultural differences in order to achieve the unity of life. For example, when Balwant Rao is sitting in the Buddha's posture, he asks Rishi, 'When you grow up and become an Englishman, will you remember me? (153). Then Rishi replies instantly, 'Don't be silly. I shall never be an Englishman. I will always live in India near Mummy and Daddy and near you and Uma. And when I am old, say twelve, I will marry Uma and you will become my brother-in-law, my *sala*' (153). Rishi's answer indicates his juvenile attachment for India and Indians and his desire for human bondage. Babu wants to clarify his doubts further, 'Seriously, you are not going to become one of those Sahebs who think that God was an Englishman, and that the Devil black?' (153). Rishi tries to convince him about the unity of life cutting across the cultural differences. He says, 'When people say God is English they only mean the word God. You have other names for God. And anyway, who knows what colour the Devil is' (153). Even as a boy of seven Rishi wants to understand the universality of life behind the apparent differences between Christian and Hindu cultures. Both of them play the game of names of God.

Though born in India, Rishi, a typical British boy exhibits the rational approach to life and questions the Hindu myths when they are not convincingly explained to him. For example, when Ramnath, a Hindu scholar and a family friend narrates the story of Lord Shiva, Parvati and Ganapati, Rishi embarrasses Ramnath by his cross-questioning, 'But Shiva cannot be a real god, for a real god knows everything and Shiva did not know that Ganesh was his son' (155). Ramnath is taken aback by Rishi's logical argument. Rishi concludes that Shiva cannot be God as God is perfect. Ramnath finally yields to him by saying, 'Yes, of course, that is so, but perhaps Shiva is an imperfect incarnation' (156). This answer seems to satisfy Rishi who is quite used to the idea of incarnation and reincarnation. Rishi's curiosity to know the Hindu gods is quite appreciable. When he asks his mother why Ganapati has an elephant head and rides a mouse, Sally clearly confesses her ignorance about it. Anyway Rishi, Uma, Hari and Sally go to Chowpatti sands and watch the Ganapati puja with great curiosity.

Rishi enjoys watching some of the typical Indian entertainment performances. Once Sally pays some money to the gypsies and arranges a show for the children. In the show, the bear Balu defeats the gypsy leader, walks on its hind legs and plays the accordion. The children enjoy the sight immensely. When Sally's encouragement to street performers is publicized widely, beggars and all kinds of artists begin to flock to her house. Once Rishi and his friends watch a play in which a four-year-old boy stands on a bamboo pole balanced on the forehead of a man. Rishi is so sensitive that far from being thrilled by the sight, he feels sorry for the poverty of India, which compels people to indulge in such risky jobs. He says, 'There should be a law to stop things like that' (160). Rishi and his friends like Babu and Uma also feel very sad. 'For a whole hour he thought that India was as poor as that, made them very unhappy and they felt aimless and unable to play, haunted by the thought that little children could be made to climb a twenty foot-long pole, not for fun but just to get something to eat' (161). Rishi not merely feels sorry for the poverty of India, but even wants to help improve the condition therein. 'It does not matter, you know, I'll live in India just the same, all my life. And perhaps I can invent something, which will make things better, like stomic food. After all I was born here, so I am an Indian too, not quite, of course, but in a way' (161).

Rishi's desire to marry Uma is quite interesting. Although Uma dreams of marrying a prince charming like Rishi and going to England, Rishi does not want to go to England and he wants to stay in India. But paradoxically enough, he does not know the meaning of arranged marriage. Then Babu and Uma explain the nature of arranged marriage, which involves the matching of horoscopes, the mediation of priests, the parental approval, settlement of dowry and the unfamiliarity of bride and groom until the wedding day. Rishi tries to understand the meaning of arranged marriages in India. After one year, there is a heavy rain and flood in Bombay. Uma and Rishi watch it with great curiosity. As a Christian boy, Rishi remembers the Biblical Flood and as a typical child with high ambition, wants to construct a Noah's arch.

Boys are normally gregarious and do not like loneliness. Rishi who is the only son to his parents, feels very lonely and wants to have a companion. 'Mummy, why don't you adopt a brother for me? There are so many little children who could be happy to come to a good home. You could easily choose one to be my brother. He could ride my motorcar and I would let him play with my mini bricks. And I would defend him against bullies, and I would not be bossy with him. Please, oh please, be a sport, and adopt me a brother. Someone like Babu' (165). His desire for a companion and playmate has a certain effect on his mother who, therefore, arranges for Rishi and the Chavan children living with each other for alternate weeks.

Like all children, Rishi enjoys picnics; sight-seeing and watching birds, beasts and insects. When the two families of Clarences and Chavans go for a three-day picnic, the two boys enjoy the experience immensely. They go to the Halfkine Institute where cobras are kept and their venom is collected for anti-venoms. They are shown microbes and germs under a microscope. On the way the children observe people fishing to honour their ancestors, as it happens to be the seventh day of Chand. Then they go to the Rocky Pool and watch the cascades at midnight and antelopes, a cobra, a wild boar, hares, monkeys and a panther.

Rishi is now seven and half years old. His parents have decided to send him back to England to join the boarding school. Before that Sally wants to shorten the duration of waiting and therefore takes Rishi to Mahabaleshwar in the high hills above Poona. There Rishi enjoys riding a pony everyday for a fortnight. Like many children, Rishi is quite mischievous, sometimes dangerously so. One day they go for a picnic where something terrible happens. When Sally roasts a marsh mellow on a stove and is about to watch a pheasant, Rishi puts a twing into the fire. Consequently the forest catches fire. They are all terrified, but fortunately the fire stops after some time. Sally's toes are blistered and her hair singed. Now Rishi realizes the enormity of his folly. 'Rishi horrified by the magnitude of his misdeed, stood on the main road, howling with terror; and even after a merciful change in the wind put an end to the forest fore and sent it back on its own ashes, he went on crying and howling' (l86). Rishi's father Peter is severely warned by the forest authorities against setting fire to the forest. Rishi's innocent mischief has dangerous consequences for everybody.

Though Rishi declares time and again that he wants to be an Indian, he has to go back to England for his education, as per the parental plan. They pack up his belongings. Rishi has to part with his close friends like Uma and Babu. Uma and Babu present him with parting gifts. Hari garlands him at the airport. Rishi is really moved by the situation and gets tears in his eyes. Sally also controls her tears, cheers him up and asks him take his school life seriously. Rishi is the only unaccompanied child on the plane. His photograph is taken before the plane takes off. Next day there is a reference to Rishi in the newspaper.

In this novel Taya Zinkin has offered a very perceptive picture of the childhood experiences of Rishi through the omniscient narration. She has portrayed different aspects of children's experience like curiosity, wonder, sympathy, ambition, dreaming, mischievousness etc., against the backdrop of colonial situation and cultural difference between Hinduism and Christianity. Rishi's identification with India and Indians is untainted by political hatred. The Indians believe that children are like gods because of their innocence and purity of mind. Rishi happens to be such a godlike child whose mind knows no barriers of race or religion, caste or creed as his heart experiences the unity of human life at every moment.

Reference

Zinkin, Taya. 1960. *Rishi*. London: Methuen & Co. Ltd.

2

Adolescence in Tsitsi Dangarembga's *Nervous Conditions*

Mary Conde

There are different kinds of education going on in Tsitsi Dangarembga's first novel, *Nervous Conditions*, published in 1988. First, there are the three kinds of formal schooling experienced by Tambu: at the local school, the mission school, and—reaching a crescendo of 'Englishness'—the convent school of the Sacred Heart. Secondly, there is the adolescent Tambu's gradual apprehension of what it means to be a woman. Thirdly, there is Tambu's very sluggishly awakening political awareness and her recognition of her uncle-benefactor Babamukuru as 'a historical artefact' (160). Fourthly, there is the growth of the articulate emotional maturity which enables Tambu to narrate the events of *Nervous Conditions* at a distance from them. Fifthly, there is the conscious education of the reader about life in colonial Rhodesia in the 'sixties and early seventies'.

Dangarembga's story of her adolescent protagonist has a very coherent pattern of imagery based on food: food seen as the means of survival, food as the mark of social status, food as the emblem of self-love, and food as a political tool. The ambiguity of the values placed on food by the characters in the novel acutely reflects the complexities of Tambu's predicament, with, as her mother puts it, "... the poverty of blackness on one side and the weight of womanhood on the other' (16). We are told in the first pages of the novel of Tambu's brother Nhamo's distaste for traveling home from the mission school by the local bus:

> He did not like traveling by bus because, he said, it was too slow. Moreover, the women smelt of unhealthy reproductive odours, the children were inclined to relieve their upset bowels on the floor, and the men gave off strong aromas of productive labour. He did not like sharing the vehicle with various kinds of produce in suspicious stages of freshness, with frightened hens, with the occasional rich-smelling goat (1-2).

Whereas Nhamo's death has already been established, in the first sentence of the novel, the food is obstreperously and offensively alive. The linking of *reproductive*, *productive* and *produce* here emphasizes not only the crude quality of survival at its most basic, which the now dead Nhamo has been trying to evade, but the villagers' function as part of a vast capitalist enterprise. Throughout this novel we are made conscious of economic necessity: Tambu's affectionate analysis of the walk home from the bus terminus—which, like the bus ride, is unappreciated by her brother—includes the opportunity for a professional appraisal of the maize crop (2), on which the prosperity of the whole village depends.

When her own family's maize crop is poor, it means that Tambu cannot continue at the local school, and Nhamo can continue only because their mother sells food which they can ill spare. Tambu, determining to grow her own maize for her school fees, is derided by her father as if she were herself a crop: 'Such a little shrub, but already making ripe plans!' It seems at this point a good omen that Tambu chooses a plot of land that belonged to her much-loved grandmother, who used to tell her stories in return for work, since her grandmother was a 'sower of seeds and reaper of rich harvests' (17).

Education, gained in return for food, is seen as a form of food in itself. Tambu's father, for example, complains that the schoolmaster Mr. Matimba thinks he can override his own parental authority because he has 'chewed more letters than I have' (24), and boasts of his brother Babamukuru:

> Our father and benefactor has returned appeased, having devoured English letters with a ferocious appetite!! Did you think degrees were indigestible? If so, look at my brother. He has digested them! (36)

On the other hand, because Tambu is a female, her father asks her witheringly, 'Can you cook books and feed them to your husband?' (15)

A superior education, in addition, literally means more food for the educated. After a year at the mission school the improved diet of the adolescent Nhamo has made him several inches taller and broader (52). And he has become food, part of 'the new crop of educated Africans' (63), set fair, like his uncle before him, to be, as Tambu says, 'cultivatable, in the way the land is, to yield harvests that sustain the cultivator' (19).

Even before Nhamo has started at the mission school, the young, Tambu, except when solaced by the camaraderie of cooking, has begun to see herself as 'no more than an unfortunate by-product of some inexorable natural process' (40). Only after Nhamo is displaced by death, a death which opens the novel and establishes Tambu's age (thirteen) and the year (1968), does Tambu move centre stage as the focus of her family's educational ambitions, no longer displaced by her femaleness.

Significantly, Dangarembga makes no attempt to explain Nhamo's death, which is presented with a perfunctory nod in the direction of credibility worthy of E.M. Forster. Nhamo complains of a pain in the neck (ironically suitable given his behaviour) and dies two days later. The suddenness of Nhamo's death appears to confirm his mother's verdict that he was bewitched by a mysterious evil: she tells Babamukuru, his uncle, 'You and your education have killed my son' (54), although there is no logical connection between the evils of education and physical disintegration as there is in Nyasha's case. This suggests that Tambu's privileged adolescent education is entirely arbitvry, caused by a hitch in the 'natural process', but that males and females alike can become fodder for the system if the caprice of fate so dictates. Dangarembga's own comment on Nhamo's death in the opening sentence was:

> When you write a novel you want people to read it. I thought I should say something stunning in the opening sentence that would focus very much on the issues I was dealing with. It has such an impact that nobody could ignore it (Petersen: 345).

Abena Busia calls it 'arguably one of the most controversial openings in contemporary African letters' (Busia: vii-viii), and another of Dangarembga's critics has observed,

> In a way, the whole novel is the story of how Tambudzai came to be capable of writing this sentence, and Dangarembga has taken some pains to wrench the novel's structure around so that it can begin with this declaration (Sugnet: 39).

Tambu optimistically sees this new phase in her life as an opportunity to rise above mundance practical considerations to an idealistic pondering of 'questions that had to do with survival of the spirit, the creation of consciousness, rather than mere sustenance of the body' (9). This is confirmed for her by the 'blaze of canna lilies burning scarlet and amber' beside her headmaster uncle's drive, 'planted for joy', as Tambu thinks, and not grown for food, for 'the chore of keeping breath in the body' (64). Later she will be similarly enchanted by the mimosa, poinsettia and roses of the convent school gardens (193).

Tambu is not, however, seduced by the mission school into neglecting the mere sustenance of her own body: she enjoys eating and becomes quite plump (95). Indeed her mother in a moment of great bitterness accuses her of having betrayed her for meat: 'Go to your Maiguru and eat sausage' (141). Mainini sees her children as cattle being fattened for slaughter (184), and it is she, like Nyasha, who voices her protest against the alienating effects of education by starving herself.

Only Mainini and Nyasha see the dangers of an education

which displaces the claims, even the language, of home. Nyasha comes to see this through her reading, Mainini, as she tells Tambu, through what she has seen happen in her own home (184). In the week before her daughter leaves for the mission school for the first time, her hunger strike is involuntary:

> She ate hardly anything, not for lack of trying.... By the time I left she was so haggard and gaunt she could hardly walk to the fields, let alone work in them (57).

Before Tambu leaves for the convent school for the first time, Mainini 'ate less and less and did less and less, until, within days she could neither eat nor do anything...' (184). She is pulled back from the brink of death by her sister Lucia, the strongest and most sympathetic character in the novel, but when Nyasha, once so healthy, 'all flour and rich baking smells' (74), succumbs to bulimia, literally flushing her vital juices 'down the toilet' (199), and she turns desperately to Tambu for help. Tambu is not strong enough or perceptive enough to save her. There is a striking analogy here with Zoe Wicomb's adolescent heroine Frieda, from the volume of short stories *You Can't Get Lost in Cape Town* (1987) who expresses her distress at being forced into a white church school by her father through neurotic overeating, and with another adolescent, the bulimic Annemarie of Elleke Boehmer's novel *Screens Against the Sky* (1990), who is effectively forced to eat cakes by her mother to dull her political and sexual longings. Significantly, the family's black servant Simon (possibly a version of Simon Peter bringing the Gospel) gives Annemarie the news of Steve Biko's martyrdom at his five o'clock meal (Boehmer: 57-60), and later drinks a Coke with her in a parody of the Communion (Boehmer: 84).

Dangarembga's title, *Nervous Conditions*, is at least in part a reference to Nyasha's bulimia. It is taken from the novel's epigraph, a quotation from an introduction to Fanon's *The Wretched of the Earth*: 'The condition of native is a nervous condition' (Sartre: 17). Fanon had characterized the settler's town as 'a well-fed town,...its belly is always full of good things' (Woddis: 26), and writes of the black man vomiting up the white man's teaching, conveying here much of the anger Dangarembga now (surprisingly) feels she has failed to articulate. Nyasha is seen throughout the novel as a counterpart to Tambu, who speaks in the first paragraph of her own 'escape' and of 'Nyasha, far-minded and isolated, my uncle's daughter, whose rebellion may not in the end have been successful' (1). Despite this merely tentative suggestion of Nyasha's destruction, Dangarembga has admitted in speaking about the novel that logically Nyasha would have to die, but 'I didn't want to do that to her.' Emotionally, Tambu goes free at Nyasha's expense.

Nyasha has, as an adolescent, no role models in her parents, since they themselves have 'precarious identities' (Sizemore: 27). She collapses mentally and physically because she perceives sooner and more clearly than Tambu the pressures of the conflicting claims on her. It is one of the great strengths of the novel that no one way of life, no one set of ambitions, is offered as the solution. Tambu's rural life is one of smoky kitchens that cause smarting eyes and permanently bronchitic chests, and 'water-drums shoes weight compressed your neck into your spine' (59). Her dispirited mother neglects the latrine, so that, as Tambu reports, 'Glistening pale maggots burrowed fatly into the faeces; the walls had turned yellow. Large bottle-blue flies with nauseous orange heads buzzed irritatingly around my anus as I squatted' (123). This description is linked, of course, to the ever-present notion of food; in an early prize-winning short story Danagarembga had already linked excrement and social privilege, the narrator of 'The Letter' says,

> You see, it was painful for me when I lived in the Township to see my mother wipe the faeces from the plump buttocks of an overfed Boer baby every hour while her children scavenged dustbins in the shanty town and had no need of the toilet for a week (Dangarembga:16, 1985).

Flora Veit-Wild says of Tambu's growing distaste for lack of cleanliness that '... the dirt fixation can be read as a symptom of the generally neurotic condition of the educated African; it finds its extreme expression in the state of anorexia'

(Veit-Wil: 336,1992). Nevertheless, the description of the latrine should certainly dispel any lingering prejudices against the modern plumbing in Babamukuru's house. Nor does rural life offer any sexual freedom. The attitude of Tambu's family, that women's needs and sensibilities were not 'a priority, or even legitimate' (12) finds its echo in the village tradition that as the girls become adolescents they are confined to that part of the river suitable for doing laundry, and are no longer able to swim 'in the deeper, cooler, more interesting pools' (3). As she grows up, Tambu is forced to recognize that there are 'bad implications' in the way she enjoys dancing (42).

But if rural life, unalleviated by any chances for travel, education or self-assertion, is presented as a trap for Tambu, so too is the alternative way of life open to her which is represented by Babamukuru's household, where the 'bad implications' in girls' enjoyment of dancing have become positively sinister. Babamukuru's traveled, educated wife Maiguru may have the same number of degrees as her husband, but she still defers to him slavishly, making a ritual, for example, of dishing up his food while everyone else's food gets cold. Maiguru does make a brief bid for freedom, but returns to her husband five days later. Although Mainini sees her as a powerful figure whose words are coveted like food (140), Maiguru sees her child Nyasha slipping away from her into death just as surely as Mainini has done. Mainini has found it difficult to talk to Nhamo because they literally spoke different languages, but Maiguru and Nyasha cannot communicate with any emotional effectiveness in that English which they both speak fluently.

Lucia, even though she is the strongest figure in the novel, still deprecates her status as an uneducated person (157), and is touchingly proud of what little education she gets (160). She may not make the mistake of getting married, but she still remains firmly imprisoned in the family framework. As for Tambu herself, while Nyasha has been absorbed in the political and historical reading which literally gives her nightmares (93), she has been immersed in fiction: Enid Blyton, the Bronts, *The Wind in the Willows* (95) and *Little Women* (177); 'Plunging into these books I knew I was being educated' (93). The only fiction we see Nyasha reading is *Lady Chatterley's Lover* (81) which is confiscated, appropriately enough for a novel about the conflict between two cultures; Dangarembga has said in an interview about D.H. Lawrence that she 'could see what he was aiming at—all the anxieties he would put in his writing' (Veit-Wild : 30, 1995). Not only does Tambu's reading have safe, harmonious endings, and advocate capitalist competition in the frankest terms, it gives back to this adolescent the reflection of English and American, not African, culture.

Nyasha's mocking of Tambu's reading as fairy-tales provides a dispiriting link with the 'fairy-tale' which Tambu's grandmother told her about Babamukuru's schooling (19), since, like Tambu's chosen fiction, it turned on reward and punishment. Dangarembga has remarked,

> Perhaps Tambudzai, given the kind of background that she had, was more at home with what could be termed myth or romance or fairy tales, with all the stories that her grandmother told her about her actual family and her ancestors, which to Nyasha would have sounded like a myth. She would have had no experience of those kinds of hardships; people traveling hundreds of miles on ox-carts and running around in loin cloths and this kind of things. So I think that's actually the tragic thing that has happened in terms of Zimbabwean history and I think that is another reason why Nyasha suffers (Wilkinson: 191).

But corruption, in the form of an exaggerated respect for literate education, seems to have infected the grandmother's narrative itself, and she is a little diminished as an admirable figure.

How far is Tambu herself an admirable figure? She constantly refers during the course of the narrative to the ways her views have changed, (*e.g.* 1, 62, 67, 116, 121, 151, 155) and much of the force of the novel depends on the journey which she still has to travel—for example, on the deadly, disarming confidence with which she tells us of her progress from finding white people repulsive to discovering that 'some

Whites were as beautiful as we were', to learning that 'they were in fact more beautiful' (104).

Tambu often indicates that she is now, as she writes the narrative, more sophisticated, and Jacqueline Bardolph has pointed out,

> The vocabulary of psychology or social analysis features more and more towards the end, when the voracious reading of Tambudzai has completely estranged her from her mother's world vision (Bardolph 40).

But Tambu also emphasizes that she is now more compassionate. She says, for example, of her brother Nhamo's hateful behaviour that now 'I have seen enough to know that blame does not come in neatly packaged parcels' (12). Above all, she presents the events of *Nervous Conditions* as a prelude. The novel ends: 'this story is how it all began' (204). The process of mental expansion which enabled her to write the narrative is, she explains, 'A process whose events stretched over many years and would fill another volume' (204). This inevitably suggests the second novel which Dangarembga was apparently about to publish, and draws our attention to Dangarembga as author and to the problems of another kind of consumption—the reader as consumer. Dangarembga has said that, despite her feelings about her 'own' language she could not have written the novel in Shona. She published her work in London because there are no women's publishing houses in Zimbabwe, and had to wait almost four years after it had been completed (Dangarembga: 44, 1991).

Speaking in June 1991 about *Nervous Conditions* (that is, a book written about six years earlier), Dangarembga said that, reading it again, 'I am absolutely shocked that I have written some things so mild—and tame. I don't know whether I am ever going to forgive myself.' She went on to say that anger permeates every aspect of the African woman's life, and that 'Publishers help you put it down that other people can manage.' The 'you' here is of course limited. As she rhetorically asked, 'How many young Zimbabwean women can write to a standard acceptable of Virago?' This raises disquieting questions about how much 'other people'—that is, the reader who is the ultimate consumer—can manage, and why? Is *Nervous Conditions*, angry though it is, manageable because its humour, its lush descriptiveness, its excitement—in short, its entertainment value—make it safe and acceptable? Is it safe and acceptable precisely because it has been made to confirm to alien standards? Nyasha, dreading her incipient total breakdown, says of her rage and grief: 'It upsets people. So I need to go somewhere where it's safe. You know what I mean? Somewhere where people won't mind' (201).

Is this a safe place for a novel?

References

Bardolph, Jacqueline. 1990. 'The Tears of Childhood of Tsitsi Dangarembga', *Commonwealth*, Vol. 13, No. 1. Autumn.

Boehmer, Elleke, 1992. *Screens Against the Sky*. First published 1990. Harmondsworth: Penguin.

Busia, Abena. 1985. 'Introduction' to 2001 Women's Press ed. of *Nervous Conditions*. vii-xiii.

Dangarembga, Tsitsi. 1985. 'The Letter' Ed. Karin Himmelshand. *Whispering Land: An Anthology of Stories by African Women Writers*. Stockholm : SIDA.

——. 1988. *Nervous Conditions*. London: Women's Press.

——. 1991. 'This year, next year...' *Women's Review of Books*, Vol. VIII, Nos. 10-11, 43-44.

Petersen, Kirsten Holst. 1994. 'Between Gender, Race and History: Kirsten Holst Petersen Interviews Tsitsi Dangarembga' (interview in Aarhus, 6 July 1991), *Kunapipi*, Vol. XVI, No. 1. Sartre, Jean Paul. 1967. 'Preface' to Frantz Fanon, *The Wretched of the Earth* (first published in Paris as *Les Dannie's de la Terre*, 1963). Harmondsworth: Penguin.

Sizemore, Christine Wick. 2002. *Negotiating Identities in Women's Lives: English Postcolonial and Contemporary British Novels*. Westport. Connecticut, and London: Greenwood Press.

Sugnet, Charles. 1997. '*Nervous Conditions*: Dangarembga's feminist reinvention of Fanon.' Ed. Obioma Nnaemeka. *The Politics of (M) Othering: Womanhood, Identity, and Resistance in African Literature*. London and New York: Routledge.

Veit-Wild, Flora. 1992. *Teachers, Preachers, Non-Believers: A Social History of Zimbabwean Literature*, London: Hans Zell.

——. 1995. 'Women Write About the Things that Move Them.' A Conversation with Tsitsi Dangarembga' (interview in Harare, September 1988) Ed.

Carole Boyce Davies. *Moving Beyond Boundaries*, Vol. 2: *Black Women's Diaspora*. London: Pluto Press.

Wicomb, Zoe. 1987. 'When the Rain Comes.' *Yan Can't Get Lost in Cape Town.* London: Virago.

Wilkinson, Jane. 1992. *Talking with African Writers*. London and Portsmouth, N.H.

Woddis, Jack. 1972. *New Theories of Revolutioin: A Commentary on the Views of Frantz Fanon*, Regis Debray and Herbert Marcuse. London: Lawrence and Wishart.

Note

Tsitsi Dangarembga's comments on the novel, where not otherwise identified, were made at the University of Gotenburg's Centennial Conference on Post-colonial Women Writers, June 1991.

3

From Infancy to Adulthood: Gandhi's Missed Childhood

Shubha Tiwari

Greatness of truth, simplicity, humility, and unpretentious narration oozes from every word that Gandhiji wrote in his autobiography. I am not a Gandhi scholar. But being in the field of literature, my fascination for this man increases on every occasion I read about him. I have no intention of idolizing him. In fact, idolizing, glorifying, and distancing of our great ones is something Indians should stop doing. There is no need to create, build, and cement the myth of Gandhi. He was a human being and therefore should be studied in this light only. Gandhi has always reiterated, '...I have all along believed that what is possible for one is possible for all...' (xii) and again, 'The further conviction has been growing upon me that whatever is possible for me is possible even for a child...' (xiv). Although this belief in itself constitutes the biggest fault of Gandhi that he thought that everyone was Gandhi, still it places him among us. And I cannot accept any distancing, any deifying, any awe, any fear for our father of nation. He is amongst us, our very own, one in our pain, and joys, our truest companion. That is how I want Gandhi to be remembered and treated. He should be a living presence amongst us.

Gandhi's narration of childhood is peculiarly amusing. Although the description is short and sketchy (how we wish that it should have been more lengthy, and detailed but perhaps he had bigger things to tell), still this picture of childhood is very revealing.

Mohan Das was a shy boy. He was a mediocre in studies. He had a heart ready to be captured by moving ideas and stories. Mohan's complete belief in what others said is very moving. When he read the stories of Shravan Pitribhakti and Harishchanra's tale of honesty, for years together he believed that these were true stories. It was as an adult that he realized that these stories were created to give lessons. From the age of roughly three to ten or twelve, Mohan was a very shy, less speaking, quite unsocial, very scared of bigger boys at school, clutching his mother's sari wherever she went, physically not very strong and quite unnoticeable kind of a boy. The magic of Gandhiji is that even as an adult he kept this child always awake in him. Every adult has a child within and it must be kept alive. Very mature, very worldly-wise, very practical kind of people may be quite successful in the worldly sense but such people may not be good human beings. Gandhiji was not such a person. Even as a big and famous man, he was child-like. About the stories of his childhood he writes, 'Still both Harishchandra and Shravan are living realities for me, and I am sure I should be moved as before if I were to read those plays again' (7). But from that mother clinging, hesitant boy, we immediately have a bridegroom ready and even eager to be married. Bapu was married at thirteen. Kasturba was the same age as Bapu. It was a group marriage—three brothers were married in one stroke, Mohan being one of them. He was eager for the fun that marriage would provide, 'Everything on that day seemed to me right and proper and pleasing. There was also my own eagerness to get married' (10). All that he thought of marriage was that he would get a strange girl to play with. But instead he got a tough girl. Kasturba had a personality of her own. While Mohan was scared to go out in the dark, he could not sleep alone, and was constantly afraid of ghosts, insects etc., Kasturba was fearless, could easily move out in the dark, and could well sleep all by herself, '...I was a coward. I used to be haunted by the fear of thieves, ghosts, and serpents. I did not dare to stir out of doors at night.

Darkness was a terror to me. It was almost impossible for me to sleep in the dark.... How could I disclose my fears to my wife, no child, but already at the threshold of youth, sleeping by my side? I knew that she had more courage than I, and I felt ashamed of myself' (19).

Mohan was consumed by the intense desire to play the husband, 'to assume the authority of a husband.' This one single factor, to my mind, tossed Mohan from infancy directly to adult world. He wanted to prove his mettle to his wife. As per the wrong Indian model of manhood where physical power, control over wife, false male authority have been unduly stressed instead of love, companionship, understanding, and sympathy, Mohan at the tender age of thirteen felt an immense urge to prove his superiority to his wife. He, at the advice of a friend, wanted Kasturba to remain at home or if move out then necessarily with someone to escort her. This restraint on Kasturba was nothing less than imprisonment and Gandhiji writes, 'And Kasturba was not the girl to brook any such thing. She made it a point to go out whenever and wherever she liked. More restraint on my part resulted in more liberty being taken by her and in my getting more and more cross. Refusal to speak to one another thus became the order of the day with us, married children. I think it was quite innocent of Kasturba to have taken those liberties with my restrictions. How could a guileless girl brook any restraint on going to the temple or on going on visits to friends? If I had the right to impose restrictions on her, had she not also a similar right? All this is clear to me today. But at that time I had to make good my authority as a husband!' (11)

Mohan also learned new ways of developing power from his friends. Meat eating, smoking and finally stealing to get cigarettes—all these Bapu did before fifteen years of age to become a man, a strong man. His friends told him that English people eat meat, they were more powerful, and that was why they were ruling us, weak Indians who were leaf eaters like goat and cows. Bapu's first experience of meat eating was very painful. He did not like the taste. He could not swallow the pieces. And the whole of that night he lived a nightmare that a live goat was crying in his tummy. Gandhiji was that sensitive. After a brief spell of enjoying meat, he finally left it in his childhood only for once and for all. Gandhiji voices the adolescent view of the supremacy of physical power very vividly. Adolescent boys have a special fascination for bulging muscles, good height and a sturdy physique. Mohan was also not free from it, 'I certainly looked feeble-bodied by the side of my brother and this friend. They were both hardier, physically stronger, and more daring. This friend's exploits cast spell over me. He could run long distances and extraordinarily fast. He was an adept in high and long jumping. He could put up with any amount of corporeal punishment. He would often display his exploits to me and, as one is always dazzled when he sees in others the qualities that he lacks in himself, I was dazzled by this friend's exploits. This was followed by a strong desire to be like him. I could hardly jump and run. Why should I not also be as strong as he?' (19) Thus in order to compete with the hardier boys, Mohan tried everything—meat, smoking and even stealing to buy cigarettes. About smoking, he says that although he could not see any benefit in the habit, yet he enjoyed the rushing of smoke from mouth, 'A relative and I became fond of smoking. Not that we saw any good in smoking, or were enamoured of the smell of a cigarette. We simply imagined a sort of pleasure in emitting clouds of smoke from our mouths. My uncle had the habit, and when we saw him smoking, we thought we should copy his example. But we had no money. So we began pilfering stumps of cigarettes thrown away by my uncle' (24).

Mohan's adolescence began somewhere around ten and ended somewhere around thirteen. That was all. His bridge between early childhood to adulthood was too thin. As a student of class sixth or seventh. Mohan was pulled by wife on one hand and studies and duties on the other, 'I must say I was passionately fond of her. Even at school I used to think of her, and the thought of nightfall and our subsequent meeting was ever haunting me' (12). I think this early exposure made Gandhiji more of a conformist, responsible type of a person. His sense of duty, although very strong in itself, was further intensified by the sense of taking care of a young and raw wife. This is clearer by Gandhiji's clear statement regarding Kasturba's education. He takes the whole discredit himself, 'I have already said that Kasturba was illiterate. I was very anxious to teach her, but lustful love left me no time.... Circumstances were...unfavourable. I must therefore confess that most of my efforts to instruct Kasturba in our youth were unsuccessful' (12). The fact that Gandhiji uses the word confess shows that he believed in the responsibility of a man in educating his wife if she like Kasturba happens to be uneducated. This traditionalistic approach, this natural faith in whatever was handed to him by generations, this simple acceptance of the running view must be due to many factors, one of them being his early marriage. In another context, Gandhiji writes, 'I was, by nature, blind to the faults of elders' (6). Another highly conformist statement comes from Gandhiji when he writes, 'I had yet to learn that all happiness and pleasure should be sacrificed in devoted service to my parents' (9). Gandhiji actually considers himself guilty of enjoying the physical life with his wife. He even relates physical pleasures to physical weaknesses, 'If with this devouring passion (for physical pleasures) there had not been in me a burning attachment to duty, I should either have fallen a prey to disease and premature death, or have sunk into a burdensome existence' (12). These are clearly traditional and wrong views. One questions something when given a chance—Gandhiji got no such chance. He was made to directly jump from early childhood to adulthood. And before he could sense anything, he was 'launched forth into public life' (12). Therefore, we do not have the carefree childhood days in Gandhiji's life. In *The Autobiography*, Gandhiji is particularly unhappy with this early marriage. He even indulges in self-pity, 'It is my painful duty to have to record here my marriage at the age of thirteen. As I see the youngsters of the same age about me who are under my care, and think of my own marriage, I am inclined to pity myself and to congratulate them on having escaped my lot. I can see no moral argument in support of such a preposterously early marriage' (7). Gandhiji also wanted to freely play, grow and develop like an adolescent! He felt that he missed that chance. Gandhiji's childhood also came in the way of developing trust between him and his wife. There is a time in every child's life when friends, good or bad, become more important than even parents and family. Gandhiji was perhaps going through this very period when he got married. His friend succeeded in misguiding him, 'One of the reasons of my differences with my wife was undoubtedly the company of this friend. I was both a devoted and a jealous husband, and this friend fanned the flame of my suspicions about my wife. I could never doubt his veracity' (23). Thus the age that should have been happy and tension free, is called by Gandhiji as 'those dark days of doubts and suspicions' (23). Another problem due to early marriage that Mohan and his brothers faced is loss of one academic year, 'Marriage resulted in both of us wasting a year. Indeed the result was even worse for my brother, for he gave up studies altogether. Heaven knows how many youths are in the same plight as he' (13). The distress of the Mahatma is very clear over having lost the opportunity of nicely utilizing his childhood days. Gandhiji, like all true thinkers gave utmost importance to childhood in the overall personality development of an individual. He writes, 'Impressions formed at that age strike roots deep down into one's nature... (31). His religiosity was much due to the fact that he was exposed to religious discourses between the ages of six to sixteen. But it is very interesting to note that Gandhiji instinctively goes for folk and rural version of Hindu beliefs rather than standardized Hinduism. For one thing, 'Samskrit... proved a harder task' (16) for him. The fact that he recited Ram Raksha in his childhood evokes this response from him, ".... I had not much belief in it. I recited partly because of my pride in being able to recite Ram Raksha with correct pronunciation' (30). His natural dislike for *Manusmriti* is very revealing about the true nature of Bapu. He was basically a follower of living, practicing Hindu ideology rather than strict laws that are supposed to have the sanction of religion. He writes, 'I happened, about this time, to come across Manusmriti which was amongst my father's collection. The story of the creation and similar things in it did not impress me very much, but on the contrary made me incline somewhat towards atheism' (32). Gandhiji's tone clearly discards the authoritative, brutal and masculine approach of Manu, '*Manusmriti* at any rate did not then teach me ahimsa. I have told the story of my meat-eating, *Manusmriti* seemed to support it.' (32) What impressed the child Mohan were Tulsi's *Ramayana* and a folk piece in Gujarati. Tulsi's soft portrayal of Ram remained Gandhiji's lifelong ideal. The Gujarati lines that struck Mohan's heart are all the more cute. This India, which is not bookish, not harsh, not other community hater, but simple, clean-hearted, assimilative—this India formed the core of Gandhiji's thinking:

> For a bowl of water give a goodly meal; For a kindly greeting bow thou down with zeal;
>
> For a simple penny pay thou back with gold;
>
> If thy life be rescued, life do not withhold.
>
> Thus the words and actions of the wise regard;
>
> Every little service tenfold they reward. But the truly noble know all men as one, And return with gladness good for evil done. (32-33)

From these lines of everyday hymns grew Gandhiji's love for "Vaishnav Jan to Tene Kahie Re" and "Raghupati Raghav Raja Ram". Community singing, as we all know, was one way of Gandhiji to cleanse hearts.

Mohan, even as a child believed in rigorous introspection. He was definitely shy. He spoke less, listened more. He was his own best critic. And this habit never left him. He had no mercy for himself; did not know how to forgive himself. This self-torturing style of Mohan can be said to be the seed of *satyagraha*. For all the wrong things, he held himself responsible. He even did not have much faith in his abilities, 'My own recollection is that I had not any high regard for my ability. I used to be astonished whenever I won prizes and scholarships. But I very jealously guarded my character. The least little blemish drew tears from my eyes.... I remember having once received corporal punishment. I did not so much mind the punishment, as the fact that it was considered my desert. I wept piteously. That was when I was in the first or second standard' (14). As can be expected from a boy of this type of nature, Mohan did not like games. All the compulsory physical training and games could not make him love cricket, or football, or gymnastics. Even the choice of exercise that young Mohan chose, is highly introspective. As we know that long, solitary walks are the best medium for an individual to create and maintain a dialogue with himself. Mohan chose this to keep fit. It is as though all the pieces of the puzzle are fitting automatically into one another. Walking is also an exercise usually associated with the elder people. Mohan's choice proves that even as a child, he felt like an adult. Childhood, or at least a vital part of it, he missed completely.

Because this Mohan was no ordinary boy, because he was to change the destiny of his land and that of other lands as well, because he was going to be loved by countless people, because his message was going to become more relevant with each passing moment, because his life was going to be his philosophy—because of all this only some tears from his father's eyes purged him for ever, ' I pilfered when I was twelve or thirteen, possibly less. The other theft was committed when I was fifteen.... I resolved never to steal again. I also made up my mind to confess it to my father.... I was trembling as I handed the confession to my father.... He read it through, and pearl drops trickled down his cheeks, wetting the paper.... I also cried. I could see my father's agony.... Those pearl-drops of love cleansed my heart and washed my sin away.... This was, for me, an object-lesson in Ahimsa' (25-26). This is by far the most touching experience of Gandhiji's childhood.

Reference

Gandhi, Mohan Das Karamchand. 1927. *An Autobiography or The Story of My Experiments with Truth*. Ahmedabad: Navjivan. Reprint 2003.

4

Revisiting Childhood in *Swami and Friends*

B. Parvathi

Childhood and children are part of imaginative literature the world over, but they receive very little critical attention except in isolated cases. However, in recent years, thanks to the new wave of thought sweeping the intellectual world, marginal areas and persons are now getting attention. It appears that epic literature in India has treated these as primary and cherished aspects of human life. In the *Ramayana*, 'Bala Kaanda' gives an account of the growing up of Rama and his brothers; in the *Mahabharata*, an account of the Kaurava and Pandava princes, also tells the sad stories of Ekalavya and Karna. These episodes of childhood, however, are integral parts of the epic. The *Bhagavatha*, which is a *purana* of the incarnations of Vishnu, in its tenth 'scandha' centres on the life of Krishna. The *Bhagavatha* celebrates the divine child Krishna whose exploits, playfulness and pranks protect Gokula from asuric onslaughts. To the best of my knowledge, the *Bhagavata* is one work which treats a delightful subject in a delightful manner. However, embedded in these several narratives are also tales of woe, deprivation, injustice and courage like that of Karna, Dhruva, Ekalavya, Anura and Garuda. The story of Prahlada, a wise, wonder-child of a demon king, is very well known to all in India. In the Indian tradition of later times, in the *Panchatantna* of *Vishnu Sarma*, the story of wayward and ignorant young princes in whom right conduct, values, distinctions between the true and false, right and wrong are inculcated in preparation for their future as rulers, is narrated. In recent times the innocence, tenderness, simplicity, wonder, happiness and brightness of childhood reflected in Rabindranath Tagore's works have become a source of joy withstanding Freud and all his theories.

After years of study of R.K. Narayan's work, the choice of simplicity as the hallmark of writing beginning with *Swami and Friends* appears to me as a remarkably rebellious trait in the writer. In spite of symbolist, modernist and nationalist influences in the air, setting the possibility of weighty themes aside he chose to write about Swami, a young boy of no distinction for his first novel.

Set in the pre-independent India of 1930s, *Swami and Friends*, R.K. Narayan's first novel, is a delightful book about childhood and children. Today after 68 years of publication, its delight increases tenfold when juxtaposed with such works as *The Beach Boy*, *The Blue Bed Spread and God of Small Things* of recent times which also focus on childhood and children. These novels often expose the distortions, thwarting and nightmarish experience that this vulnerable age can be subjected to turning the joys of childhood into a myth. But thanks to R.K. Narayan, revisiting childhood is still possible and delightful.

One can only fully agree with Prof. K.R. Srinivasa lyengar who wrote: 'It is as though everyday actuality has taken Narayan's pen and written out this universal epic of all our boyhood yesterdays that are now no more' (*Indian Writing in English*: 365). *Swami and Friends* is a tale of 'growing up', difficult for the boy but delightful for the reader who is led into the bylanes of harmless hassles and memories of childhood.

The first child with none to boss over, Swami takes the centre stage at home although he is too young to know it. Extremely unselfconscious that he is, his likes and dislikes are clear. Sunday is a sweet, heavenly day to him—Monday and school following in its wake take the shape of a minor misery.

Swami enjoys ample freedom at home except for occasional checks by father. He is loved and cared for tenderly although very unobtrusively. He would have enjoyed the company of friends and classmates at school fully but for geography, arithmetic and Ebenezer, the scripture master. School for him is not only a place for the company of friends and play but also teachers and punishment. In this place Swami feels vastly superior to the 'untidy', 'tiny', 'leg swinging', 'bench sitting', 'ill clad' toddlers of infant standards. He does not understand why the tiny fellows should come to school to make clay elephants, mangoes etc. which can be made easily at home also. To Swami schools are meant for serious things like geography, arithmetic, English and the Bible. He prefers the company of senior boys and teachers but for their formidable looks. Swami, the young boy is simple enough to wish his friends see him riding in a car.

Swami hardly spends any time thinking about life because it means for him the secure presence of father, mother, grandmother and home and he takes all of it for granted. His impatience with grandmother is characteristic of the impatience of the young for the old. He loves her but tells her quite frankly that she is old. The possibility of grandmother dying of stomach ache waiting for the lemons she asked him to get worries him and makes him feel guilty. To his relief fortunately, granny is quite alive and also relieved of stomach pain. His thoughts mainly centre round school, friends and teachers. Affections, relationships and discovering life alone preoccupy his attention. Like home, money is another matter which he takes for granted. During holidays Swami falls in love with the idea of acquiring a 'hoop'. He dreads to wake up to a 'hoopless morning'. He dreams of playing with it; the hoop turns into a horse in his dream and gallops with Swami on its back. A hoop costs money and money is a scarce commodity especially for a child like Swami. From where would he get the two annas which the coachman's son demands? Mother and grandmother do not handle the household's finances; father worries over running the house for the month with the money left in his purse and Swami wonders what father did with all the money his clients gave that he cannot spare two annas! Father, on another occasion, looking at Swami's preposterous examination requirement list admonishes, 'Do you think rupees annas and pies drop from the sky? Swaminathan did not think so but something nearly so' (*Swami and Friends* : 59). Even the 'mighty Mani's' helplessness in money matters comes as a matter of great surprise to Swami.

Therefore, Swami resorts to practicing something like alchemy to make money! He puts some pebbles in a cardboard box, covers them with fine sand and leaves, and prays to god to turn them into money. He puts Lord Rama — the ten-headed — demon-slayer's divinity to test with his prayer to turn the pebbles into money and also promises to give up biting his thumb for a year! To the boy's disappointment the pebbles remain as pebbles. His anger at the gods turns into fear. He wants to abuse the gods but thinks better of it because he 'might get on without money but it was dangerous to incur the wrath of Gods.' So the cardboard box with pebbles receives a reverential burial. Thus, the story of the hoop, in spite of Mani and Rajam's best efforts, ends in a fiasco because of the coachman's son.

Except for Mani, Swami's attachment to his friends remains purely intellectual, *i.e.* confined to school. The miniscule enacting of dramas of the adult world occurs in the jealous accusations of Mani and loud protestations of Swami regarding Rajam which, resolved in a confrontation between the old and new friends of Swami, ends in a new friendship making him feel 'at perfect peace with the world.' Swami's affinity grows stronger for Mani and Rajam in the following days. The description of their first visit to Rajam's house is quite amusing for its transparent simplicity, fear, eagerness and innocence. When a policeman in uniform outside walks towards them 'Swaminathan felt like running and fleeing.' Even Mani the mighty (who had to sneak out of his house) is actually afraid of the man though he tries to cover it up with excessive casualness. Rajam keeps them waiting for a few minutes in imitation of his father; but with friends in the adjacent room, biting nails does not please him for long. Are the friends hungry? Their reply is a half hearted 'no'; but the ease and authority with which Rajam commands the cook invites their wonder. When he over does the role and the cook carries away the food tray, an admiring Swami expects Rajam to shoot the disobedient cook with his gun. He is simple enough to expect Rajam to shoot his defiant, disobedient cook, and naive enough to believe that Rajam really kicked the defiant cook into unconsciousness.

Rajam — the police superintendent's son, the boy who comes in a car to school, the boy who regularly secured seventy percent who speaks English like an Englishman, the boy from Madras, 'is not ordinary' in Swami's view. Rajam also becomes 'killer of tiger' in Swami's account to grandmother. Moreover, Rajam does not only have a room for himself but also a study table and such 'a young fellow to own a timepiece on the table' gets more of Swami's admiration. Swami's invitation and arrangements at home for receiving Rajam show his eagerness to impress his new friend with a show of equal status, attended by the cook, good coffee and interesting tiffin instead of the usual insipid variety which he usually gets. Anxiety lest things should go wrong nags him. It is not surprising, therefore, that Swami tries to impress Rajam passing off father's office room and table as his to the amusement of the latter. He worries about his old grandmother talking drivel to Rajam. To him a sleeping grandmother seems safer for display. Fortunately to Swami's relief Rajam's visit goes smoothly except for the cook who does not wear a clean dhoti. Swami's intimacy and natural fondness for Mani and Rajam extends beyond school. Their bond is stronger when compared to other friends. Mani, Rajam and Swami spend most of their time together in the holidays.

Swami's very good friends are an interesting lot; Sankar is an intelligent boy who can outwit the masters; even the teachers respect Somu, the 'uncle' of the class; Samuel 'the Pea' giggles with Swami over the most trivial of things, and Mani the 'mighty' who has been attending school ever since the old peon could remember, who comes to the class goes to the last bench and 'slept bravely' boasts about settling scores with his strength and wooden clubs. However, the first bitter taste of peer disapproval comes to Swami because of his fondness for Rajam. Somu, Sankar and Samuel nickname Swami as the 'Tail' of Rajam as a result of which in the class 'Not a word reached Swaminathan's brain, in which there was only dull pain and vacuity'. Yet the same Swami demonstrates qualities of heart quite unmistakably be it the case of being called 'the Tail' for which he fights with Samuel and Sankar their friendship notwithstanding; their group wins a new, mature and generous friend in Rajam whose efforts close the schism in the group. Rajam delivers such a sermon about punishment in hell that it reconciles the bitter enemies to friendship. Of course, he also tops the sermon with announcement of gifts for each one as a reward for reconcilement.

The arrest of Gauri Sankar on 14th August 1930 in Bombay leads to countrywide protests, Malgudi included. On this day the rebel, non-conformist, adventurer and impressionable mischief-maker in Swami comes out. In the meeting on the bank of Sarayu, a Congressman addressing the people recalls India's greatness in the past and its present condition. His words about England 'no bigger than our Madras Presidency and is inhabited by a handful of white rogues and is thousands of miles away' subduing Indians impress Swami. The congress worker's exhortation, 'Let every Indian spit on England, and the quantity of saliva will be enough to drown England...' stirs something deep within him. 'Gandhiji's jai' shouted Swaminathan involuntarily, deeply stirred by the speaker's eloquence at this point. The remark of the leader 'spit on the British' and drown them' plunges his mind into pondering over the possibilities of such an act for getting rid of them. If driving out the British was that easy why it is not done puzzles him. The Congress worker's description of British atrocities, exampled in cutting off Dacca muslin weavers' thumbs etc., infuriates the young lad to become riotous — a stone pelter, pane breaker; and active participant in the bonfire of foreign cloth. The small boy decides to mete out punishment to the offenders of Indian weavers by wearing only khaddar, the rough homespun. He turns to Mani to find out of what cloth his clothes are made of! On the whole, on the 15th of August, Swami goes to bed with a painful head tapped by a police lathi, bruised hands and legs, loss of 'khaddar' cap and an aching body. He feels very sorry that the protesting Malgudians should be dispersed under the orders of his friend Rajam's father, the police superintendent! The following day at school the Headmaster takes Swami to task for mischief of the earlier day. Swami is normally a passive boy but the pain in his legs, head and back emboldens him to defy Headmaster's caning. 'Every pore in Swaminathan's body burnt with the touch of the cane. He had a sudden flood of courage, the courage that comes of desperation.' He fights the rushing tears, grasps his books and rushes out of the school saying, 'I don't care for your dirty school.' His refusal to go back to Albert Mission School surprises his father who admits him in the Board High School.

Rajam, at first unforgiving, later comes to Swami with the idea of a cricket club, an idea translated into reality which further complicates Swami's simple life with misunderstanding and misery. He is no cricket enthusiast in spite of familiarity with big names like Bradman, nor does he think much of his ability to play cricket. Now a student of the Board High School, Swami shows more loyalty to friendship with Rajam and the newly found Malgudi Cricket Club than to the discipline of the new school. Swami and friends play and discuss cricket till late in the evening. Punishment from the drillmaster at the Board High School once again leads to him to defy and run away from school and home. Finally, he loses his way into the Mempi forest to the great anxiety of his family and despair of the Malgudi Cricket Club which loses the cricket match to the Y.M.U. For some reason, Rajam from the beginning can think of nothing except of things going wrong, of defeat and worries about the match and his fears come true. The cricket match leaves for Swami the wrath and loss of a dear friend ; and for Rajam defeat and disappointment.

Swami is a happy, sensitive and imaginative boy, a loyal and accommodating friend capable of getting into a mood of protest and defiance. His realization about the mistake in not confiding in his father about the Scripture teacher, his participation in the bandh, his commitment to cricket, his resolve to run away from Malgudi to Madras or Bombay, yet come back for cricket match and his agony over Rajam indifference may be small incidents in an adult world but these are very real and almost tragic for the sensitive young boy except that they are immediately corrected or alleviated. He gets into trouble for a cause outside his self — first the bandh and later cricket match for which Rajam calls him a 'peculiar fellow'. Unlike Rajam, he is capable of being inspired by imaginative, unknown and larger issues. The assured security of home protects him from the shocks Estha gets or the abuses of *The Blue Bedspread* — from the distortions of negligence and the depravity of adult world.

Swami and Friends will continue to fascinate readers in print and also viewers of the small screen because of the visual impact created by Doordarshan. The novel's place among classics to the world about children is well assured.

References

Narayan, R.K., 1932. *Swami and Friends*. Madras: Indian Thought Publications.

Iyengar, Srinivasa, K.R. 1990. *Indian Writing in English*, Madras: Asia Publishing House.

5

Adolescent Sensibility in Mahasweta Devi's Short Fictional Narrative *Bayen*

Madhu Singh

Literary texts from almost all cultures and societies are replete with adolescent characters, depicting their likes and dislikes, their traumas, their mental agonies, even their rash and raucous dispositions. Adolescent behaviour has been diagnosed and analyzed from psychological standpoint and, therefore, belongs to the realm of psychology. A number of psychologists have done seminal works in this direction. Of late, adolescent psychology and behaviour has also been the domain of literature, the sufficient evidences of which can be obtained in the fiction of Charles Dickens. Pip in *The Great Expectations*, Oliver in *Oliver Twist*, David in *David Copperfield*, Little Nell in *The Old Curiosity Shop* are some of the finest specimens of adolescence.

If we delve deep into these characters, the common points which emerge can be broadly stated as follows: the youth is most of the time rash, chaotic, impulsive but informed with elan, vigour and vitality. An adolescent is very often identified with teenagers and refers to young, juvenile, minor stripling youngster. In other words, 'adolescence' means time in a person's life between childhood and mature adulthood. This is the transitional period between puberty and adulthood in human development, extending mainly over teen years and terminating legally when the age of maturity is reached.

Mahasweta Devi, acknowledged as a foremost Indian author, is rapidly achieving world class stature. Her writings have received enthusiastic critical responses and have been seen from a number of different perspectives such as feminist, subaltern, peripheral, radical, Marxist and so on and so forth. However, the adolescent sensibility, which is more or less implicit in one of her short stories, *Bayen*, has not been explored by the critics. The present article aims at exploring adolescent sensibility and the trauma that an adolescent undergoes because of the harsh treatment meted out to him in the name of oppressive and outdated social values and obsolete tradition. Bhagirath in *Bayen* is one such sensitively drawn adolescent character who despite being an insignificant character is psychologically oppressed and hence deserves our sympathy and attention. The only other character that can measure up to the level is the little Hamid in Premchand's short story *Idgah*.

The first impression that one gets about Bhagirath is that of an ordinary young boy, a character that does not seem to promise much to the overall development of the plot. But as the story comes to an end, he emerges into a powerful and moving persona arousing a lot of admiration and sympathy. Before analyzing his character and accounting for his adolescent behaviour, it is important to present in brief the chain of events through which he emerges into a powerful character. In the process, attempts will be made to account for the reasons, which lead to the separation of mother and son and the indelible strain that it leaves behind on the adolescent, which he cannot remove by any kind of corrective action. The only way remains open is to embrace the dignified mode of suffering and the ultimate sacrifice, which the mother does at last by killing herself, emerges into a universal dimension. The redeeming grace of the story lies in her suffering, the effect that it creates on Bhagirath and the pathos that Mahasweta Devi creates through unique paradigm of words and images. In the story the invisible social structure with its obsolete and outdated values appears as a villain and proves a blocking stone on the emotional bond of sympathy that exists between the mother and the son.

Bhagirath inhabits a desolate and cheerless universe right from the very beginning, where all is befogged, baffled and constricted by evil. He was very young when his mother was declared a witch and thrown out of the village. Despite her genuine love for her child Bhagirath, which can only spring out of a mother's heart, his mother dare not look at him because she has been conditioned to believe that 'she has but to cast her eye on a young man or boy and she would suck the blood out of him. A *bayen* has to live alone, see no one' (8). Her maternal instinct, thus, gets suppressed under the sheer oppressive deadweight of an outdated tradition, which is hackneyed, moth-eaten and flawed. The motherly, nurturing, caring, affectionate, tender, doting, material instinct becomes martyr to these unjust patriarchal assumptions. We seldom come across such a precarious situation in literature. The pathos, the agony and the poignancy of feelings are not only intensely moving but also plaintive to a great extent.

Set against the barbaric practice of witch-hunting or witch branding, Mahasweta Devi 'evolves an intensely human story, touches the larger space of the social forces that separate mother and son in a male-dominated system' (Bandhopadhyaya: xii). The most dominating character of the story is Bhagirath's mother, Chandidasi Gangadasi, who was 'a keeper of the cremation grounds' (16) and a descendent of legendary Kalu Dom who had given shelter to the great king Harishchandra when he had lost his kingdom.

When the narrative begins Bhagirath is a thirteen-year old school-going boy, son of Malindar Gangaputra, a *dom* by caste who had a government job in the subdivision margue 'that entitled him to forty-two rupees a month' (10). Bhagirath was raised by a foster mother as his own mother had been branded a witch and *thrown* out of the village. So, deprived of maternal love at a very early age, he never knew what a real mother was like. As a child, he would occasionally catch 'the reflection of the red-clad figure (of the *bayen*) in the pond, a sun bronzed face framed by wild, matted hair and eyes that silently devoured him' (9) without knowing that she was his real mother. As he saw her image 'in the dark waters' (9), he would shudder violently, close his eyes and cling to his father. Once when he saw his father speaking to her, he was very frightened and disturbed because 'to talk to the *bayen* meant certain death' (10) and he did not want his father to die. He questions his father: 'You, you talked to her, Baba? Malidar said, his voice growing somber, 'She may be a *bayen* now but she used to be your mother once' (10). This shocking revelation that the *bayen* was his mother leaves him cold and shaken. How could he believe that a *bayen* was also a human being after all! To quote :

> A *bayen* for a mother! Is a *bayen* a human being then? Hadn't he heard that the *bayen* raises dead children from the earth, hugs and nurses them? That whole trees dry up the instant a *bayen* looks at them? And he, a live boy, born of a *bayen's* womb? (10)

The mother-son relationship once established and confirmed arouses in him fear-mixed curiosity and a previously unknown emotional affinity towards her. But he dare not approach her for fear of never coming back alive, if he did, he could be turned into a tree or a stone forever. Once assured by his father that she would never do *him* any harm, his mind rushed to the rail-side where Chandi *bayen*, his mother lived alone in a hut under the tree, a red flag fluttering on its roof. He would quietly watch her from afar without being noticed only to see how terror stricken the *bayen* was of her loneliness. 'He had a mad wish to rush to the hut, then afraid of his own wish, he swiftly traced his way back home' (12).

One day while walking along the railway tracks, Malindar took his son's hand and said, 'Why should you not know what everyone knows about your mother?' (14) Then, he narrated the whole life story of his mother in a voice choked with emotion. As the story came to end, both of them heard the far off sound of the *bayen* singing:

> A strange strain of music floated up to them from afar, accompanied by the beat of a tin can. The song seemed to have no words at first but gradually the lines became distinct. Bhagirath knew the song. His stepmother sang it

to put her daughters to sleep. The song entered his soul, mingled in his blood and reverberated in his ears like some incurable pain. (22)

A dazed Bhagirath returned home. But a few days later he rushed to the dead pond at noon. The shadow of the *bayen* trembled in the water. She did not look at him but kept her eyes lowered while filling a pitcher with water. The following scene between the mother and the son and the dialogue that takes place, the first ever to happen, captures that poignant moment and freezes in our imagination:

'Don't you have another *saree*? Would you like a *saree* that is not torn as this one is? Want my *dhoti*?'

The *bayen* was silent.

'Some nice clothes?'

The son of Gangaputra had

better go home.'

'I go to school now. I am a good boy.'

'I am a *bayen*. Even my shadow is evil. Doesn't the son of Gangaputra know that?'

'I am not afraid.'

'It's high noon now. Young children shouldn't be out in this heat.'

'Aren't you afraid to live alone?'

'Afraid? No, I am not afraid of anything.'

Then what makes you cry?

'Me, cry!'

'I have heard you.'

Her crimson shadow trembled in the water. Her voice cracked as she said, 'Let the son of Gangaputra go home and swear to come near the *bayen*. Or.... I will tell Gangaputra!' (22)

Bhagirath saw her turn back and race along the mud culvert, 'her hair swirling about her, her crimson cloth fluttering in the air' (23). He sat along for a long time by the pond, till the waters became still again. He could not recall the song. The link that he had tried to establish with his mother had snapped. Despite her maternal love and concern for her own child, it was she who severed the tie and 'felt a very wifely anger at Malindar' (23) who had failed to protect Bhagirath from the witch's eyes. This was the first and the last time when Bhagirath could interact with his mother.

The same evening she found the notorious Gourdas and his gang piling up bamboo sticks on the tracks to stop and loot 5 Up Lalgola Passenger which was carrying Wednesday's mailbag with a lot of money. In order to avert the accident and save the lives of the passengers, she runs along the track towards the train waving at it wildly. 'She continued to scream in order to stop the train till the roar of the train drowned her voice and the train's light swallowed her up' (24). This act of martyrdom and supreme sacrifice pulls down all superstitions and prejudices woven around her as a *bayen*.

The Railway Department announced a medal for her to be awarded posthumously to her closest survivors and invited someone to claim the award. Everyone was silent. People looked at one another and scratched their necks in embarrassment and looked down. Finally someone whispered, 'Yes sir, she was one of us' (25). This statement astonished Bhagirath so much that he looked from one face to another. He realized that his community had recognized her at last.

Then follows an intense scene full of raw emotional energy. Bhagirath, till now a young boy, seemed to grow up overnight. Like a true son, he rises up to the occasion to clear his mother's name by claiming the *bayen* as his mother. He says:

> My name is Bhagirath Gangaputra. My father, the revered Malindar Gangaputra. Residence, *Domtoli*, Village Daharhati...my mother...' he paused and then, very distinctly, 'my mother the late Chandidasi Gangadasi....' Bhagirath broke into loud sobs....' My mother, the late Chandidasi Gangadasi, sir. Not a *bayen*. She was never a *bayen*, my mother. (25)

The officer stopped writing and stared first at Bhagirath, then at the crowd. The *doms* 'stood silent, eyes downcast, like people condemned. The silence was suffocating and unbearable' (25).

In a provocative study of American post-war fiction, Richard Ohmann has traced a recurrent leitmotif in some leading novels dealing with adolescent sensibility. He says:

> The person hanging onto childhood as the only defense against capitalist and patriarchal social relations is most often a man or woman already implanted in an adult role but only masquerading as a productive and well adjusted member of society. In other words, the rite of passage marked by illness and movement towards recovery may be, and usually is, an adult crisis' (Molesworth: 1031).

It is surprising to note that American fiction is conspicuous by its easily recognized adolescent social misfits. American fiction has a long tradition of such adolescents ranging from Huck Finn to Holden Caulfield. The adolescent sensibility cloaked in an adult role finds expression in some leading American novels such as *One Flew over the Cuckoo's Nest*, *An American Dream, The Bell Jar* and *Herzog*. This technique of camouflage allowed the post-war novelist a way to mediate the powerlessness of individuals in a mass, post-industrual society with the continuing belief in the power of the single, sensitive personality (Molesworth: 1031).

In all these novels, it is important to recall that the suffocating social fabric chokes the adolescent characters longing for a better life.

Mahasweta Devi in *Bayen*, makes a significant departure in treating adolescent sensibility. Unlike American post-war novelists, she portrays not only the victim of the unjust social order but also its practitioners. Her depiction of adolescent psyche emerges into a powerful critique of decaying social values and traditions and the direction of our social development since independence.

References

Devi, Mahasweta, 2000. *Bhiku's Diary and other Stories*, Geeta Dharamrajan ed. Mahua Bhattacharya, trans. New Delhi: Katha.

Devi, Mahasweta, 1997. *Mahasweta Devi: Five Plays*, trans. Samik Bandhopadhyaya, Calcutta: Seagull Books.

Molesworth, Charles. 1988. 'Culture, Power, and Society'. *Columbia Literary History of the United States* Elliott Emory ed. New York: Columbia University Press.

6

Depiction of Childhood in the Autobiographies of Indian Women Writers

Alka Saxena

Childhood is usually associated with fond and happy memories of the days gone by. The child is ignorant of the hassles of adulthood and enjoys her/his carefree days, but childhood memories may not be so exciting and wonderful for everyone. The aim of the present paper is to study the autobiographies and biographies of some women writers and examine the gender discrimination they experienced during their childhood days. Let us delve into the past of some firebrand and glamorous women writers and see for ourselves how they recount their childhood days in their memoirs. The autobiographies of Kamala Das, Shobhaa De, Sharanjeet Shan and other women writers reveal the social stigmas which are attached with the birth of a girl child.

My Story is a compelling story of Kamala Das, one of the most controversial Indian writers today. Though her autobiography is remembered for the candid revelations she had made of her married life, but what concerns us here is the recollection of her childhood days. Kamala Das confesses that she was ordinary-looking. As a child of nine she was made conscious of her dark complexion. Her grandmother was worried about the duskiness of her skin and rubbed raw turmeric all over her body before the oil bath. Her grandmother oiled her hair and washed it carefully with a viscid shampoo made out of the tender leaves of the hibiscus. It was fashionable then to have curly hair and naturally she took pride in showing it off to her relatives who praised her thick tresses but mumbled unkind words about her colour.

Her father found her to be too rustic for his liking. So Kamala was admitted to a boarding school run by the German Catholic nuns. Kamala was given proper education but her father was quite orthodox. When Kamala made her trip to Malabar, she was not accustomed to wearing a saree. But visiting her orthodox relatives down south, she had to wear clothes that hid legs fully, for ladies at Nalapat were conservative, puritanical and orthodox.

In her grandmother's home at Nalapat, Kamala met Robbin Das. When she was a child she had met him several times. But now it was different. Her grandmother considered that he was a very good young man as he had no vices. Even her parents felt that Kamala should get married soon. She was fifteen at that time. Her father wished to retire and settle in Malabar. As he had not yet fulfilled his duty to marry his daughter he was very troubled. Kamala Das has commented. 'I was a burden and a responsibility neither my parents nor my grandmother could put up with for long. Therefore with the blessing of all, our marriage was fixed' (Das: 82).

She returned to Calcutta after her engagement. Her mind was perplexed. It was clouded with doubts. She wondered if she had been reckless in accepting the proposal. Her friends in Calcutta were shocked to hear of her engagement. She was still a child and needed to complete her education before thinking of getting married. But since all was fixed by her parents, nothing could be done. Her life had been planned and it's course was charted by her parents and relatives. While the preparations were going on, Kamala ran and played with children all over the garden. Soon a young child bride became the victim of a young man's carnal hunger. The wedding was only a show of wealth. Her parents took pride in displaying and proclaiming that they had spent half and a lakh on its preparation.' The bride was unimportant and her happiness was a minor issue. There was nothing remotely Gandhian about the wedding. When Kamala Das remarked on the extravagance, she was scolded by her grandmother who said, 'You ought to feel grateful to your father for arranging such a lavish wedding for you. Go up to your room and rest there. I do not want the relatives to think that the bride is a tomboy. (Das: 87).

Soon after her marriage she realized that her husband had married her for her father's social status and the possibility of financial gains. Marriage had become a trap for the child bride who soon became the mother of a boy. For sometime, Kamala Das stayed with her parents. When she finally went back to Bombay to her husband's home, her life became miserable because of her husband's carnal hunger.

The biggest tragedy was that Kamala Das could not admit that her marriage had failed. In our society a broken marriage is not approved of. She knew that she could not return home to her Nalapat house as a divorcee. 'My parents and other relatives were obsessed with public opinion and bothered excessively with our society's reaction to any action of an individual. A broken marriage was distasteful, as horrifying as an attack of leprosy. If I had at that time left my husband, I would not have found it possible to find another who would volunteer to marry me, for I was not conspicuously pretty and besides there was the two year-old who would have been to the new husband an encumbrance' (Das: 102).

Thus the girl's childhood was sealed with an unhappy marriage. There was no one to share her misery and pain. In such circumstances she took to writing. Soon her poems were accepted by the journal *P.E.N.*

Selective Memory is an engaging candid memoir of Shobhaa De, the glamorous model turned magazine editor, columnist, T.V. script writer and author. Here De writes poignantly of her earlier years and of her relationship with her parents and siblings. She writes, 'Unfortunately for my mother I was not a second son she had prayed for. My birth could not possibly have been a day of celebration for the family especially since my maternal grandmother was around to remind everybody that a third daughter had arrived as an additional liability and it had been rather reckless of my parents to have gone in for a fourth child with no guarantee that it would be male. Whether or not my mother had really and truly been moved to tears of dejection at the nurse's announcement of my sex, my grandmother had made sure she felt wretched and guilty about it. As she began to cry tears at the sight of me, her mother had slapped her own forehead hard in an unambiguous gesture of disappointment' (De: 12).

It was only Rao Saheb, Shobhaa's father who rejoiced on seeing the perfectly formed infant. He consoled his wife by telling her that God had been kind to them by giving such a healthy and good-looking daughter. About the same time the wives of Rao Saheb's peon and orderly each delivered boys and for the great achievement they were clearly one up on him. Mr. Rao was a special magistrate, a high ranking official but now as the father of three daughter his status was lowered. While from the servants' quarters the triumphant cries of mugla! (boy), mugla! arose, there were at the same time gleeful references to poor Rao Saheb's mugli (girl). There was a gloomy sadness at home. When Shobhaa's elder sister Kunda who was six at that time, rejoiced at the arrival of her new sister, she had no idea that it was only the birth of a son that called for celebration in the family. Kunda was also considered inauspicious in comparison to her elder sister Mandakini. Mandakini's birth was followed by the birth of a son Ashoka. Due to this Mandakini had an auspicious *kumkum* hand impression imprinted on her back, to commemorate the birth of her brother. After the third child Kunda, Shobhaa a girl was born, so Kunda was also considered inauspicious. She had to face her grandmother's scorn and wrath. Her grandmother rebuked her saying, 'What! You want *kumkum* on your back? Go and fetch some cow dung instead. Do you realize there are three daughters in the family now? Weren't two enough?' (De: 20)

Fortunately for the family many changes for the good happened after the birth of Shobhaa, so she was considered lucky for the family. Thus, the initial feeling of being let down by the daughter's birth was transformed to warmth and love soon after.

In her memoirs, Shobhaa De has referred to an incident of sexual abuse she experienced as a child. The incident happened when she was ten years old and her father's colleague came to visit them at home. She writes 'I can still see the expression in the eyes of one particular man when he asked me to lead him to the washbasin to clean his hand. While I waited holding a hand-towel, this man who was in his mid-forties made a crude pass, pretending it was an accidental touch. But I recognized it for what it was and fled. Seeing my expression my mother asked me what had happened. I narrated the incident and watched her face crumple with horror and disgust. She whispered something to my father, who abruptly declared the dinner over. The man was never invited back' (De: 22).

Shobhaa's parents were very much concerned about the activities of their daughters. She attended school and took active part in athletics. As she had to wear shorts for such sports, it was met with her father's disapproval. But at last he relented on the condition that shorts should be worn only on the field. Shobhaa was a different kind of a girl right from the beginning. Gradually, she took interest in modeling and when her photo featured on the cover of *Femina*, her father was really disgusted. He said that modeling was not a career for a decent girl and did not approve of this line.

Shobhaa De shares memories of her first pregnancy in her autobiography. She admits that during her first pregnancy, she was told by someone that if a woman glows and looks wonderful, it means she will have a daughter. On hearing this Shobhaa stopped blooming. Unconsciously the pressure of producing a son got to her. She began worrying that if her first born would be a girl, it would bring disappointment to the eager family. The birth of her son Aditya is remembered very emotionally. There was great celebration within the family. The social conditioning is so deep-rooted that even modern women like Shobhaa De fall prey to social pressures of having a son as their first born.

While examining the autobiographies of women writers from the point of view of assessing their childhood days, Tiwana's *A Journey on Barefeet* is a relevant memoir. Although Tiwana's account is essentially personal, yet her struggle is the struggle of every woman. Several concerns of women such as dowry, women's education, the general preference for sons and the status of women form an integral part of the story. Dalip Kaur Tiwana is a sensitive and prolific writer who has several short stories and novels to her credit. Her autobiography *A Journey on Barefeet* received the Gurumukh Singh Musafir Award in 1982.

Tiwana was born into a traditional family of rich and prosperous Zamindars. Her life was a constant struggle right from the beginning. Tiwana remembers her mother as a neglected woman in the family because she had not given birth to any son. There was no one to carry the name of the family. Her mother was a woman with a dark complexion and she unobtrusively attended to the various household chores. Due to her dark complexion and not giving birth to any son, she was the most neglected woman in the house. Tiwana's aunt, who had been married for quite some time, did not have any child. Tiwana's uncle had married again with the hope of getting an heir, but even the second marriage was fruitless. So Tiwana was sent away to live with her aunt. To the disgust of her grandmother, a third daughter was born to Tiwana's mother.

Now that there were three daughters in the house Tiwana was taken away by her aunt. Almost everyone in the house rebuked Tiwana's mother when a third daughter was born to her. Her grandfather consulted a purohit ji and asked him to find out some way to have a son. He was worried over the spate of girls born into the family. Grandfather also wanted to know if the same wife will bear a son or will his son have to marry a second time.

Tiwana's grandmother never spoke gently to her daughter-in-law. All the time she was reprimanding her in some way or the other—'What good are you if you cannot give us a son' (Tiwana: 17) or 'Oh God its our bad luck that you have fallen to our lot. That bride of the peepal tree house took no time in giving birth to two sons in quick succession. A lucky family indeed! And you' (Tiwana: 17).

Her grandmother prayed under her breath for a grandson to be born whose light she would be able to see in her lifetime. Tiwana's father was a drunkard and this was also a cause of concern for the family. They wanted a son so that the property could be given to him. Once again the discrimination between a son and a daughter in legal affairs is highlighted. Tiwana and her two sisters could not have a rightful share in their father's property. The birth of a son was therefore necessary.

It was after many years of prayers that a son was born in the family. Tiwana at last had a brother. Her mother who was doomed otherwise, was given some respect once the son was born. At least now no one could blame her of not bearing a son. Grandmother lavishly distributed wheat among the poor. Many other gifts were also offered.

Tiwana records in her autobiography another problem which is usually faced by girls in our society. Tiwana recalls the time when her marriage was settled. When a couple of months were left for the wedding, the parents of the boy broke off the engagement. In Tiwana's house the preparation for the marriage had started on a hectic note. Amidst such joyous atmosphere when the proposal was called off, the family was left astounded. The social stigma that a daughter in the family had been rejected was upper most in the minds of all at home. Tiwana's self confidence was shattered. She would stand before the mirror and have doubts over her looks and appearance. She wondered if she was bad looking.The rejection of a daughter for marriage after it had been settled was a very serious matter. It would affect the prospects of Tiwana's two younger sister as well. Years later Tiwana's aunt brought another proposal. But this time her aunt was too sarcastic in her words, 'What belongs to the garbage dump must ultimately find a place there. Girls can't live in their parent's homes all their lives. They must go where they belong. Here's a good opportunity coming your way. Of course, you can try in other place. Nobody can stop you from doing that. But they would all insinuate that she is a once—rejected girl, you may find yourself at a dead end' (Tiwana: 89).

Thus, in Tiwana's autobiography the familiar issues of gender discrimination are acutely felt. The psychological trauma that a girl undergoes after her marriage is called off and the social reaction to such incidents is genuinely expressed.

Sharanjeet Shan's autobiography entitled *In My Own Name* is a recollection of the continued struggle she underwent right from childhood. Her life-story exhibits extraordinary courage, faith and determination. From childhood, Shan had a mind of her own. She chafed against the restrictions of her status as a girl, subject the authority now of her father, in the future, of her husband. In the preface she writes, 'My book is merely a narration of the tragic events of a bright young girl's life; a life that was transformed, indeed cut short because of the orthodox marriage system. It is a statement of a very personal mental anguish, on behalf of hundreds of women I met, while working on this book, in various centers and battered wives homes up and down the country, Asian women in particular. It is a statement of agony on behalf of the many hundreds of girls who go through the same trauma even today. She states that as a nineteen year old student she was trapped in the web of tragic circumstances born out of cultural and traditional dogma. Recounting the time of her birth, she writes that was my beginning to Sardar Ajeet Singh and Bibi Pritam Kaur, a daughter, born to be *parai*, (someone else's property).

'What a pity! The first child should have been a boy; remarked the Muslim midwife' (Shan: 6).

Shan's brother was born a year and a half later. Her mother and grandmother were always busy around Paramjeet. For some peculiar reason he always seemed to need more attention than Shan. It was much later that Shan came to realize the importance of a son to Indian parents. If anything had to be shared, she was told to be a good sister and let Paramjeet, her brother, have it. She was made to believe that she must have done some good deeds in previous life to have been blessed with a brother. Her parents were keen that she should study but alongwith this they also made sure that she did all the household chores. From the age of seven, it was Shan's duty to clean the floors.The fact that Paramjeet should always receive preferential treatment, specially from their mother was accepted as a norm by Shan. He was encouraged to play and take part in a number of extra curricular activities, while Shan was confined increasingly to the four walls of the house. Shan's interest in fashion was severely disapproved and criticized by her father. There were no such restrictions imposed on the brother. Her mother would secretly feed Paramjeet on goodies and apples, almonds and Vitamin enriched milk drink as Horlicks and Ovaltine. It was considered vital brain food for him as he had the task of carrying on the family name, while not once was any such health giving food ever kept aside for Shan. If Paramjeet ever shared this food with Shan, he was scolded and asked not to spoil his sister as she was 'a parai' and so she must learn to suppress such temptations.

Shan was amused to hear her mother sing 'My son will grow up to be a king one day.' She was amused by such a curious prediction. She wondered that if all the sons in India would take up the throne one day, there was bound to be a glorious mess. According to her father, it was 'Bure Karam' bad deeds of past lives, which caused one to be born a woman or to a schedule caste. She often felt confused about her role as a daughter. She makes the following observation in the chapter, *Born to be 'parai'*, 'On the one hand a daughter was referred to as Devi (Goddess), while on the other she was always being looked upon as a burden, a temporary guest, a duty to be discharged. It was almost as if the reference to Devi was made in order to cover up a kind of guilt the parent might feel for having given birth to daughters. Amongst people of all the three major religions that I knew within our acquaintance, a woman was greatly honored as a mother of sons, especially by the in-laws while a mother of daughters was ridiculed by relatives and friends alike. The biological truth that it is the father who decides the sex of the offspring is ignored, I never understood. From the moment a daughter was born to the day she was married, one heard of nothing but the whole family's preparations and the sacrifices that would have to be made for the dowry to make a suitable match. As a result, a daughter invariably feels guilty for her very existence' (Shan: 13).

Similar events are described in Mrinal Pande's *Daughter's Daugther*. It is a cluster of sensitive reminiscences. It is a book about growing up as a girl. Gender discrimination was felt by Mrinal Pande in the very early years of her life. The childhood experience of Pande are quite similar to those which are recorded by other women writers in their autobiographies. *Daughter's Daugther* is about the darker side of childhood. In the Author's Preface, Pande writes, 'I know, even as I write this, girls are being destroyed in wombs by new techniques, being tortured and burnt for dowry.... No, survival is not easier for our young girls today than it was for us.'

Most of the events recorded take place in her grandmother's home, where her being the daughter's daughter was always a disadvantage. All the attention was paid to her cousin, Ann, who was the grandson. Their grandfather would often treat Anu to a slice of mango or toffee but the daughter's daughter, *i.e.* Dinu and Tinu were deprived of such favours.

Mrinal Pande often heard derogatory remarks about girls trying to get education. Her aunts were of the opinion that girls eventually needed skills only to roll out *chapattis* and do the cooking. It was feared that education would make the girls vain. The experiences of her childhood days made Mrinal realise that men were the icing on the cake in her grandmother's house.

She also saw the sorrow of her mother, Shivani, who had three daughters and pined for a male heir. It was much later when Pande grew up, that she was told by her mother that she had cried herself to sleep on the night her third daughter was born. The grandmother's grief was even greater, for the third daughter was born in her house. Her grandmother looked pityingly at Shivani as she expected her fourth child. The anxious relatives called Prakash, a cousin, to predict the sex of the unborn child. He made a sign of a money box with his hands which clearly meant a boy. Girls were bad cheques, they were like auctioneers decrees. Boys brought in money, land, gold, everything. Girls just took away things' (Pande: 83). Mrinal Pande remembers the day when her brother was born. Her mother looked so relieved and relaxed. Everyone was happy that now the brother will protect the sisters and carry on the family's name. Her grandmother hugged the youngest granddaughter who had brought a brother on her back. A large cake of jaggery was placed on her auspicious back. Mrinal Pande has described these events as stories about the survival of a daughter's daughter. While going through the account of childhood experiences of notable women writers a common pattern emerges. The gender discrimination is very evident and obvious. The preference for a male child, the pity for a mother of daughters, the different set of morals made for boys and girls have always existed in Indian society. Biographies of eminent women like Indira Gandhi and Kiran Bedi also recount such events. Kiran Bedi's encouraging biography enlists some strong convictions which can change the future of girls in the new millennium. Bedi believes that as long as women continue to be in a position of receiving rather than giving, they shall continue to bear injustice. She remarks that women have to develop the will and determination to constantly review their situation. Only then will the men share resources with them. With more women coming in, the situation will change. Thus, in order to give a happy childhood to girls, an unbiased social perspective and a change in social attitude is required.

References

Das, Kamala, 1976. *My Story*, New Delhi: Sterling Publishers.

De, Shobhaa, 1998. *Selective Memory*, New Delhi: Penguin Books.

Tiwana, Dilip, 1990. *A Journey of Barefeet*, New Delhi: Orient Longman.

Shan, Sharanjeet, 1991. *In My Own Name*, New Delhi: Rupa and Co.

Pande, Mrinal, 1993. *Daughter's Daughter*. New Delhi: Penguin Books.

7

The Girl Child in Indian Novels in English

Sharada Iyer

Jean Jaques Rousseau, the champion of human struggle for freedom stated 'in children we must allow childhood to come to its own fulfillment.' He was of the view that children should be children before they become adults. Rousseau's prescription has no hope for the girl child. She is deprived of the limitless joys of childhood experiences which implies growing up before one's time. This impression is strengthened when one reads the ancient Indian literature. There are no girl children as leading characters or for that matter, a character making its presence felt. Girls did grow up to be important characters as in the epics, but it was not felt necessary or worth lingering on their childhood phase. They were of interest only as young women to play the role of beloved, wife and mother.

The opening statement of Tagore's novel *Inauried* classifies women into two categories—the first who are primarily mothers and sisters and the second who are beloveds or wives. It is obvious that in this world of mothers, sisters, beloveds and wives there is hardly any place for the girl child. They step straight into adulthood and are expected to be responsible and wise. Very often the little girl becomes 'little mother' before she even learns the meaning of childhood. It appears that the Indian baby girl immediately graduates to adolescence, not even adolescence but the bashful young womanhood and quickly to the courageous long suffering figure of mother.

In the literature of the recent past we have been greatly concerned with the have-nots, the downtrodden, the untouchable and women. But when we look for the girl children one is disappointed that not much has been written about them in a significant way. Childhood considered so important as a period for the formation of character and for the emergence of value structure, has largely been ignored as an area of human experience where girl characters are concerned. This reflects both a literary and social reality.

The neglect of the child's experience, details of its response to the environment, within the family and outside, remains more pronounced in the case of the girl child than boys. In a few examples where fiction/stories have used the consciousness of a child to portray the world as seen from its perspective, the child is generally a male. There are no counterparts to Jane Eyre, Maggie Tulliver, Little Dorrit, Flora or Pearl. At least Oliver Twist, Huck and Tom have their counterpart in Mulk Raj Anand's Bakha in *Untouchable*, Munno in *Coolie*, Swaminath in *Malgudi Days*, Bunty in *Aap Ka Bunty*. Even when a girl makes her appearance, her presence is patterned on submission and subordination. She is an invisible silent presence. In Gangadhar Gadgil's short story *The Lost Children*, Manisha's fate is the fate of the typical girl child who is never cuddled or appreciated, who is blamed for everything that goes wrong, who is never a child but always a woman.

The mind, personality and the experience of the girl child are closed within parenthesis. Girls are a silent part of the family. What a girl thinks or feels about this social eclipse does not interest the writers. She is like a cipher that acquires value only when a numerical digit is added to it. The most formative years of woman's life—while she is growing—remain by and large unexamined and unexplored.

'The literature of the early 20th century had numerous girl characters between the age of two to ten, but they appear either as child wives, prospective brides or widows and seldom as little children. In her book *The High Caste Hindu Women*

Ramabai pointed out 'Childhood is the heyday of a Hindu Woman's life but as almost all the girls are married before they are twelve, these happy days of freedom are few in number'. Sarat Chandra—the apostle of the downtrodden women and an incisive and sensitive author who could penetrate into every layer of woman's psyche, too deals with the adolescent woman, the young woman as mistress, wife, sister, courtesan or rebel with rare insight but the girl child does not hold his attention. As an exception we have Bibhuti Bhusan Bandopadhyaya's *Pather Panchali* which gives a detailed study of Durga, a six year old girl and her brother Apu. A naughty girl perpetually busy with her childhood games, she roams about freely, her hair wild and unkempt, her hands and feet unwashed, creating mischief wherever she goes. Durga occupies a very small part of the novel, she dies very young. We see her through her little brother Apu's eyes.

However, the Indian novel in English has redeemed the gloomy situation by creating some memorable girl children. Notable among them being Kamala Markandaya's *Two Virgins* where the main characters are two young sisters Lalitha and Saroja, Raka in Anita Desai's *Fire on the Mountain*, Tara and Bim in *Clear Light of the Day*, Sarita in Shashi Deshpande's *The Dark Holds No Terror*, Jaya, Mander and Veena in *That Long Silence*, Estha and Sophie Mol in Arundhati Roy's *The God of Small Things* and Evie Jamila and Tony Catrack in Rushdie's *Midnight Children*. We do come across some delightful delineations in the writings of Ravindra Nath Tagore, R.K. Narayan and Kamala Das on which this paper is focussed. They too recognise that children have a way of creating their own spaces.

Tagore himself put sufficient efforts towards the collection of doggerels and rhymes which he felt would give a true picture of the life of women in Indian society. He tells tales of child marriage, child abuse, marriage of little girls to old men, the ill treatment by in-laws, polygamy, desertion, starving and torture. In his short stories he has captured the girls in their diverse moods and experiences. He wrote stories during almost all the period of his long career. 'Tagore is the first writer of the true story in Bengali and he has remained the best,' wrote Sukumar Sen. The stories reveal Tagore as having a remarkable insight into the psychology of children, their joys and sorrows, their hopes and disappointments. Their success and failures are portrayed with a masterly touch which makes them alive in his pages. Tagore's stories are a poet's effort at fiction, hence share the glory and limitations of the source of origin. The myth making power of Tagore is best illustrated in 'Kabuliwallah' in which the character is seized by inward vision and presented with total understanding and love. The child sees the Kabuliwallah with the eyes of trust and affection and so the beast becomes the beauty and the stranger becomes a friend. In due course the child Mini who is incapable of wasting a minute in silence becomes a bashful girl. With a few deft touches, Tagore suggests the miracle of the buds unfoldment as the full blown flower. Tagore lavishes his art especially on children and women and presents them not realistically but poetically. The child's innocence, wisdom, fragility, helplessness, her beauty, all provoke the poet, while the efficient storyteller merely records the laugh, the sighs, the murmur and the cry.

Tagore's vision, though romantic is perceptive and unfailingly captures the nuances of Indian girlhood. In 'Kabuliwallah' the touching friendship between the vendor and the little girl is given a poignant twist when she is to get married and the usual question playfully asked embarrasses her, 'When are you going to your father-in-law's house'. The word 'father-in-law' is an euphemism for prison. The Kabuliwallah unfortunately goes to the prison after a brawl, returns after years to meet his little friend Mini, 'May I not see the little one, Sir, for a moment?' He had a small gift for Mini. With great difficulty over ruling all objection of a bride being presented to a stranger, Mini arrives and she is now ready to go to her father-in-law. The ramification are further humanised when the Kabuliwallah suddenly remembers the daughter he had not seen for so many years and wonders whether she too with the onset of womanhood, would not be lost to him. Tagore is mature as a storyteller in 'Kabuliwallah'. He introduces a narrator, the main character is Mini, a little girl of great charm and wit. A very human story is built around her. Tagore's stories show a wide variety of situations, which gives expression to innocent jokes of 'Kabuliwallah'. 'Little one, will you go to your in-laws place' to the wry humour in 'The Wife' where the school teacher bullies Ashu for playing with dolls like girls, to the sardenic laughter of 'Taraprasanna's Achievement' where the wife is guilty of having given birth only to daughters, the rude ridicule of the child bride who tries to preserve a small diary in 'Exercise Book', and the death of the child bride due to ill treatment by the in-laws in 'Give and Take'. Tagore uses an overall ironic framework to expose the moral ambivalence, malice and hyprocrisy that has prevailed in a cowardly society. There are however, a few pieces which deal with the playfulness of little girls, their naughtiness, and love of freedom. However, their unbounded joy is hinted as being more becoming in boys. In most of the stories, there is a strange transformation in the end, all the girls turn into obedient and loving wives either of their own free will or due to the forces of circumstances.

Children are instinctive, they have strong imagination, vivid sensation, they see life as black or white, bigger than reality, their enemies seen as demons, their friends angels, their joys or sorrows absolute and eternal. Naturally it is not easy to survey the world from the standpoint of children. Only writers like Dickens, who are gifted with intense imagination and exceptional genius can point convincing pictures of childhood like he did in *David Copperfield*, *Great Expectations*, *Oliver Twist*, and *Little Dorrit*. It is highly creditable that R.K. Narayan in his very first novel *Swami and His Friends* has shown such an extraordinary understanding of child psychology. The plot revolves around the activities of a group of school boys, Swami and his friends Mani, Shankar, Somu, Samuel and Rajam. In this novel he gives a vivid and comprehensive account of the activities, thought, nature and life of school children. The author's understanding of child psychology is so perfect that his portrayal of the child world is as authentic as it should be. There is hardly anything about child life which has not been revealed. Like Wordsworth he seems to say ‘ The fullness of your bliss, I feel, I feel it all’.

Narayan displayed a deftness and insight in the handling of children. He had a soft corner for little girls as he romanticises most of them. Seetha in ‘The Birthday Gift’, Shanta in ‘Forty Five a Month’ are fine portraits of little girls. They are realistic, sweet and at times manipulative. Narayan’s fondness for the rare skill in portraying child characters, especially little girl child is visible in ‘English Teacher’ as well.

Leela in ‘The English Teacher’ is a lovely portrait of a three year old girl. It is the most autobiographic of his novels. Narayan himself wrote ‘More than any other book, *The English Teacher* is autobiographical in content, very little part of it being fiction.’ The English Teacher, Krishnan is a fictional character in the fictional city of Malgudi but he goes through a similar experience as the author. He calls his wife Sushila, and the child is Leela instead of Hema. The toll that typhoid took and the desolation that followed with a child to look after and the psychic adjustments are based on his own experience. The book falls into two parts. One is domestic life and the other is spiritual. The second part of the novel knits smoothly together Krishnan’s devotion to his daughter and it is hard to put it down in plain language his efforts to recover his connection with his dead wife. The child, Leela, whose personality is tiny brilliant mirror of her mother’s image keeps the mother’s presence from fading away. It is characteristic of Narayan to sink the general into the particular and emotion into action, that the growth of Krishnan’s love for the little girl is seen through his increasing mastery of the delicate skill needed in tending a young child.

Thus, we see that Tagore and Narayan wrote on the girl child in an era when attention was showering on male children. Their approach may be traditional, their vision for the girl child may be bound by home walls but their pure love for this girl-child figure cannot be questioned.

8

The Theme of Pre-Adolescence in Modern English Fiction — A Bird's View

Purnima Mehta

One of the interesting phenomena in modern English fiction is the persistent recurrence of the theme of childhood. To name a few important writers, James Joyce, Katherine Mansfield, D.H. Lawrence, Virginia Woolf, Compton Mackenzie, Hugh Walpole, Forrest Reid, A.L. Baker, Richard Hughes, Joyce Kary, William Golding, Graham Greene have written fiction with conspicuous focus on childhood. It is perhaps Henry Reed who first noticed with casual interest the phenomenon of the recurrence of the theme of childhood in modern English fiction in his booklet the *Novel Since 1939* (1946). Another novelist-critic, P.H. Newbly, makes a few speculative suggestions in his book *The Novel 1945-1950* (1951), explaining the attraction of the theme of childhood to twentieth century writers. Peter Convey's *Poor Monkey* (1957) which is mainly a study of childhood literature in the nineteenth century deals with pre-adolescence fiction in the early twentieth century. William Walsh is of the opinion that major writers of the nineteenth century excel those of our day in the power with which they perceived and communicated the life of the child.

It is with Dickens that childhood is established as an important theme in English fiction. *Oliver Twist* (1938) is the first novel in English with an exclusive focus on pre-adolescence. Dickens's concern with childhood is seen in half a dozen more novels. We also find childhood treated with particular interest in Frances Trollope's *Michael Armstrong* (1840), Charlotte Bronte's *Jane Eyre* (1847), Mrs. Gaskell's *Mary Barton* (1840), Charles Kingsley's *Atton Locke* (1850), George Eliot's *The Mill on the Floss* (1860) and *Silas Marner* (1861). Stevenson's *Kidnapped* (1886) and Mary Corelli's *The Mighty Atom* and *Boy* (1896 and 1900). We might also mention here Kipling's short stories like, 'Baa Baa Black Sheep'.

The concept of the child on which the Victorian fiction of pre-adolescence is generally based is essentially derived from Rousseau on the one hand and the romantic poets, Blake, Worksworth, Coleridge on the other. Rousseau is the first serious thinker to give considerable thought to the study of childhood and education. He emphasized that the original nature of the child was innocent, and that childhood has its own ways of seeing, thinking and feeling. The romantic concept of the child has corollary that the child's remarkable qualities are lost as the child grows. It is the domain of poetry that the child first entered and that in the 1440 it established itself in the novel. The romantic vision of the child appears 'all-right' in poetry, but when this vision is expressed in terms of fiction, the result is idealised, sentimentalised and consequently unreal characters of pre-adolescence. Thus, the child in Victorian fiction is rather a personification of the romantic concept. The second striking thing about them is the note of pathos that is usually evoked in them. They are the victims either of poverty or shabbiness or of willful cruelty. The pathos of childhood is intimately connected with the social concern of the Victorian novelists. There is very little or no attempt to depict children from the inside. The reason is obvious, the Victorian novelists were not interested in children as children but as a means to evoke pathos, as a means to contrast the evils of society with the innocence, goodness and helplessness of the child. The tender lips of small children converse on subjects like religion and philosophy. The Victorian fiction of childhood is, on the whole, 'fiction' in the sense it is rarely on a realistic natural plane. Childhood is rarely depicted for its own sake, and on its own level. It is interesting to note that the children who are successfully depicted have an autobiographical origin. It was left to the twentieth century to delve deep into the already discovered continent of childhood and depict it with astounding insight and objectivity.

There was one outstanding and exceptional attempt in the nineteenth century to put the child in the right focus. Walter Pater in his long story called 'the child in the house.' He speaks for instance of the little insignificant things like the large attic, the shadow of streets, the illustration in the old big *Bible* at home that act on the child's fancy and become part of the texture of his mind. He even speaks of stream of impressions anticipating in a sense William James' stream of thought of consciousness. Though, perhaps, it fails as a story, *The Child in the House* is a pioneering attempt in the nineteenth century to focus attention on the child's mind and the process of his growth.

Published in 1903, Samuel Butler's *The Way of All Flesh* reveals a definite reaction to the child. His attitude to childhood is remarkably free from sentimentality and idealization. But Butler's main interest is to expose the nineteenth century family life and educational system. The credit of blazing a new trail in the treatment of pre-adolescence goes unquestionably to Henry James. He is the first novelist who consciously faced the problem of depicting the child's mind. James' method to articulate what is almost inarticulate in the child's experience is certainly valid and legitimate.

From 1910 onwards we find a number of writers treating childhood with conspicuous interest. In the wake of Freud and Adler a lot of psychological work appeared. There is, normally, an intimate relationship between literature and environment. The twentieth century has been an age of continual crisis and consequently an age of disintegrating values. Most writers felt alienated and isolated in a society which was more or less atomized. Hence, they turned inwards. Now from the point of view of the pre-adolescence theme, inwardness might become escapist and result in nostalgia.

Henry Reed gives nostalgia as the reason for the recurrence of the childhood theme in modern fiction. Moreover, a writer faced with 'a world of darkness' may turn to childhood not only nostalgically but with a serious intention of searching for human values. Joyce Cary tries to do the same in his *Charley is my Darling*, *A House of Children* and *Castle Corner*. Cary says that his main concern as a writer is to search for 'human constants', he then says:

> The innate feelings of a child may be said to belong to a world of university forms.

In Joyce Cary we have a peculiarly twentieth century attitude—that of exploring childhood in order to search for human values. William Golding made a similar attempt in *Lord of the Files* to understand civilization in terms of the miseries and cruelties of a group of children marooned on an island. The child in modern fiction is no longer a sweet, innocent, helpless, harmless creature but he is a bundle of impulses, a raw soul, mixture of sensation, facing life, struggling to comprehend it. Forrest Reid's portrayal of child's mind is traditional and straightforward. Mansfield's style is impressionistic. In her best work *Prelude*, *At the Bay*, *The Doll's House,* the attitude of healthy nostalgia is found. In her allegorical stories *How Pearls Button was Kidnapped*, *A Suburban Fairy Tale*, she uses the child as a critic of society. While L.H. Hartley's main artistic interest is in the essential drama of childhood, *i.e.* The Go—Between.

Basically, their attitude can be divided into egocentric and those which are objective. Katherine Mansfield and Forrest Reid represent primarily the egocentric attitudes and Joyce Cary and L.H. Hartley represents mainly the objective attitudes.

On the whole, the world of children is depicted as world by itself, unique and apparently autonomous. Hence, children are hot miniature adults as in Victorian fiction. Modern fiction of pre-adolescence should be of great value to educators. It has acquired a distinct place in modern English literature.

REFERENCES

Walsh, William. l995. 'The Writer and The Child' in *The Use of Imagination.*

J.J. Rousseau. 1762. *Emile.* Ed. Barbara Foxley, Everyman's Library, London. Reprint 1911.

Arlingtopn, Richard ed. 1948. *Walter Pater's Selected Works.* London: William Heinemann Ltd. Reed, Henry, 1967. *The Novel Since,* 1939.

Cary, Joyce. 1958. *Artand Reality,* London: OUP.

9

The *Panchatantra* and *Aesop's Fables* in the Reader's Mind

Sadhana Agrawal

A fable fascinates and excites the reader. It occupies a prominent place in the world of literature. As soon as it is narrated, the reader enters into an exciting and thrilling world where only improbable things happen. The young and the old, the cultured and the illiterate, everyone succumbs to the spell cast by the fable. All those for whom moral values reign supreme, the *Panchatantra* and *Aesop's Fables* still have no match in influencing and changing the reader. Even 'In an age of computer games and Cartoon Network, children's book are surprisingly still in vogue...' (*TOI*, April 18, 2003). Books influence the mind of the children and help the growth of their personalities. How do the fables act on the mind of the reader? What is their purpose? From where have they come down to us? These questions deserve answers. This study focuses attention on the two representative and influential works of the hoary past, namely the *Panchatantra* and the *Aesop's Fables* and makes an attempt to prove by comparing them that fable is an important form of literature and its impact on the mind of the reader is immense.

For a number of centuries, the stories and the fables were told orally. They were preserved in the memory of the people till written versions emerged. The 'oral art of tale-telling is far older than history, and it is not bounded by one continent or one civilization. Stories may differ in subject from place to place, the condition of tale-telling may change as we move from land to land...', rightly observes Smith Thompson. A question may come to the mind of the reader that since modern writers have ceased to write animal fables, such a study does not serve any purpose. In reply, it can be pointed out that the 'PC-at-Home' revolution a few years ago witnessed a surge in the sale of computer games and compact discs, but gradually people are going back to books. Educationists attribute this to awareness among parents about the detrimental effect of the visual medium on children. Hence the animal fable is not so extinct as it is believed to be. It will continue as long as animals do. Aesopian tradition is still continued in the colour comics of Walt Disney's *Mickey Mouse and His Friends* and that of Hannah Barbera. The readers are still interested in animal fables.

Although the fable is one of the important forms of literature, it is a pity that very few scholars have paid any serious attention to this form. There are some limitations in such a study that must be pointed out so that no misgivings arise. This study will help to recreate the total literary situation whose visible crystallization is a work of art. Although the time of either *Aesop's Fables* or the *Panchatantra* cannot be pinned down with any certainty, reconstruction of social history is not aimed at. A general description of that state of culture or ethos which makes animal fables possible will be focused in brief. We can say nothing with certainty but a few things can be guessed by studying the textual evidence. Nevertheless, the *Panchatantra* have some characteristics of the oral tradition. The boxed structure of the *Panchatantra* and isolated simple stories of wisdom of Aesop naturally are an index of the length of time.

Aesop's Fables and the *Panchatantra* assume the existence of a system of stock animal characters, each invested with a certain human quality—fox for cunning, the hare for timidity, the dog for fidelity and the donkey for foolishness. Such a tradition of stock animal characters and thus telling a tale can be traced back to primitive stages in the development of the human being who lived in thick forests surrounded by wild beasts of forests and birds of the air and had a close contact with them. So it was but natural for him to invent imaginary animals and to make them act and speak like human beings. This might indicate that the fable originated at a time when people were nature-worshippers and believed that all which lived and grew had souls or spirits. Sainte Beuve is right when he says. 'Had this view of things not been evolved by the primitive man, nobody would have invented the fable in a civilized society.' No doubt, living there she started telling tales, expressing hopes and fears, beliefs and ideals to amuse and give solace to people. It can be assumed that the animal character was born out of the most primitive hunting man's experiences. They will last as long as there are readers to read and listen. They have living roots in a soil that is as fresh today as it was in the time of earliest civilizations.

William Hazlitt is of the opinion that 'Man is a poetical animal and delights in fiction.' It suggests that love for fiction making faculty is inherent in the nature of man. Whereas Aristotle is of the view that Man is a social animal. And so he is compelled to tell others his experiences. An experience is shaped into various forms of literary art. One of them, the oldest of all literary activities we are dealing with here, is the fable. Crabbe defines the fable as follows: 'The fable is allegorical, its actions are natural, but its agents imaginary.'

Smith Thompson defines the fable as follows: 'When the animal tale is told with an acknowledged purpose, it becomes a fable. The best known are the great literary collections, *Aesop*, and the *Panchatantra*. They usually attach an actual maxim, though this is not necessary. But the moral purpose is an essential quality, which distinguishes the fable from other animal tales.' *The Oxford Advanced Learner's Dictionary of Current English* defines the fable as 'a short story that is intended to teach a moral lesson. Fables are not based on fact and often have animals as characters: *Aesop's Fables*'. And the *Standard Dictionary of Foklore, Mythology and Legends* puts it: 'An animal tale with a moral; short tale in which animals appear as characters talking and acting like human beings though its purpose is the pointing of a moral.'

The definitions given above mean that the fable is a short narrative, each animal and bird is endowed with the speech and action of human beings, and the fable is followed by a moral lesson. Brevity is an important characteristic of a good fable and it leaves much ground for the reader's imagination. The other features depend on it and arise from it, as we see in the fables 'Dog in the Manger' and the 'Goose that Laid Golden Eggs'. Because of the brevity of the form, it cannot be told in length. It must, therefore, hit the nail on the head. The characters are mostly animals, birds and inanimate creatures. These characters stand for certain qualities. Thus the courage is identified by the lion, greed by the wolf, cunningness by the fox and foolishness by the ass. They talk and behave as if they are given man's intelligence in a certain degree. Each animal and bird is endowed with the gift of human speech and action.

There is no reason why the animal appearance and animal behaviour could have conditioned these conceptions. We can understand the ferocity of the tiger, the kingship of the lion, faithfulness of the dog and the stupidity of the donkey. Hence the stock character of an animal has become a part of the linguistic idiom. But a lion is not always wise — he is outwitted by a hare, not noted for its cleverness. The intended teaching in the story of an old lion who is living by the tributes of his own subjects is that the king should be active. No animal enters the mouth of a sleeping lion. Such a tale derives from not only a political existence, but also one peculiar to India—the Mandala polity in which Kautilya's *Arthasastra* and the *Panchatantra* of Vishnu Sharma are based.

The stock character is often transgressed, altered and reduced to present some special quality, which it represents itself. A free character is thus born, it is individualized and plays a particular role for a particular situation. The fable of the *Monkey* and the *Crocodile* is the best example of it where the monkey plays an unusual role, which is against its instinctive behaviour. The Crocodile in the *Panchatantra* is first shown to be clever enough to deceive the Monkey, but gives himself away by talking boastfully. The Monkey invents a characteristic of its species — it leaves its heart on the top of the tree. And the foolish Crocodile takes him back to the bank of the river and lets him jump up to his tree. He is fooled. It is totally a drama of bourgeois existence. Thus the main beauty and spell of the animal tale lies here. It makes the animal tale a genre, a human drama. The animal fable is still alive in the reader's mind and is enjoyed not only by children but also by adults.

A good fable is followed by a moral lesson, which is in keeping with the tone or tenor of each story. The moral maxims are usually in the form of proverbs that are very easy to remember, as: 'A stitch in time saves nine,' 'Sour grapes', 'Unity is strength,' 'Like father, like son,' 'Stoop to conquer', 'Might is right', etc. In *Panchatantra*, the maxim, which contains the moral, is usually in the form of a verse, as:

na tatha badhyate loke
prakritya nirdhano janah,
yatha dravyani samprapye
tairvihinah sukhe sthitah.

('A man born poor does not suffer so much affection in this world as does he, who, having obtained wealth and lived in happiness, is deprived of it afterwards.') (Translated, verse 92, Tantra II).

India has a rich collection of well told stories which are found in the epics like *Mahabharata* and *Ramayana*. The *Jataka* stories told by the Buddha are similar to the fables in the *Panchatantra* and the *Hitopadesa*. The *Brihatkatha* written by Gunadhya in the Paishachi language is the earliest collection of stories and fables but the original work is not to be found now. We agree on all hands that the original work from which the Sanskrit version of the *Panchatantra* and also the Kannada version of the *Panchatantra* derived are the *Brihatkatha* of Gunadhya. It consisted of stories recited by Shiva to Parvatidevi. This shows that the stories have come down to us from an immemorial tradition and that they were current amongst the common people who spoke not Sanskrit, but Paishachi, the natural language of those considered to be low in those days.

Neither *Panchatantra* nor *Aesop's Fables* is available in its original form. Many of the Fables of Aesop are obtained from ancient authors prior to the time in which he lived. It appears that Aesop did not writc his fables. They were spoken as occasion gave rise and where handed down from mouth. A collection of *Aesop's Fables* compiled by Denetrius Phalerum about 300 B.C., is not available now. Babrius made first Greek version of *Aesop's Fables* but the exact place and period in which he lived is yet undetermined. Avianus compiled forty-two fables about 400 A.D. in Latin verse. A number of collections of *Aesop's Fables* available in English and French are based on stories coming down to us from the classical Greek sources.

The biographies of Vishnu Sharma and Aesop are in much obscurity. Vishnu Sharma was a Shaiva-Brahmin and Aesop was a slave. Vishnu Sharma had wild and young princes to serve whereas Aesop did not have any such purpose. Both had a stock of popular animal stories. A study of both the *Panchatantra* and *Aesop's Fables* unfolds a number of similar stories. But the more we compare the Greek and Indian fables, the more we recognize the close similarity between popular opinions of the two men on all ordinary questions of practical wisdom. However, much difference there may be between the manners and customs of the two nations, there is a wonderful agreement between the judgements arrived at in India and in Greece on matters of everyday life. Regarding this, Mahatma Gandhi observed, 'Keep on recording these stories for they are ambassadors between the East and the West.' It may be of interest to note that 'India is the classic land of fable, allegory, parable and story. No where in the ancient world did these forms of art flourish in such luxury and variety as in the land between the Himalayas and the Sea.' And Dr. Winternitz rightly remarked: 'It is not, therefore, too much to say that life is indebted to India for fables.'

The *Panchatantra* that touches the innermost part of the heart of the reader and influences her/his mind wholly contains five *tantras* or sections called *Mitrabhedam, Mitrasampraktikam, Kakolookivam, Labdhapranasham* and

Apareekshitakarakam with an introductory section called the *Kathamukha* which gives a view on the background of the work. First of all Vishnu Sharma, the author of the *Panchatantra*, invokes the blessings of the Gods so that no *impediment would come in completing the work*. The story of the *Panchatantra* begins with the name of a country in Southern India, Mahilaropya where Amarashakti, the King of the country, has three sons called Bahushakti, Ugrashakti, and Anantashakti. All the three princes are dullards and averse to all learning. Here Vishnu Sharma classifies the bad sons into three classes—the son belonging to the first class (not born at all) is the best one and the one belonging to the third class (the son who is dead) causes grief to the parents only once, and the son of the second class (the son who is a fool) causes grief at each and every step.

The King is naturally too much worried about his sons, as they are dullards and so seeks the advice of his pundits. Sumati, a minister of the court, devises a royal road to learning. 'Verily the science of words is of unlimited extent; life also (on the contrary) is short, and the *obstacles* many: its essence, therefore, should be taken (grasped, mastered) leaving out what is worthless, as milk is drawn out of water by swans.'

Sumati then recommends Vishnu Sharma, the Brahmin Pandit, to whom the King invites to coach his sons in the art of running a kingdom and in general how to gain success in life. In return the king promised to pay a hundred land grants but Vishnu Sharma replied: '*Naham vidyavikrayam shasanshatenaapi karomi*'. Translated 'I am not the man to sell good learning for a hundred land grants.' Vishnu Sharma then undertakes to teach and make the princes masters within the period of six months. He devises a new technique to instruct the youths through the fables. In the *Panchatantra*, he tells the importance of the work. 'Whosoever always studies this science of politics or hears it (reads to him and acts on it) never suffers a defeat even at the hands of Indra who is never thwarted in his pursuits.'

The *Panchatantra* instructs *niti*, worldly wisdom, and the art of running a kingdom and in general, of success in life. In India, the term *niti*, *tantra* and *yukti* are used with a wide spectrum of connotations. From 'polity' upto 'morality' they vary according to context. All the meanings, quite often, co-exist. The *Yajnavalkyasmriti* speaks of a conflict between the *Dharmasastra* and the *Arthasastra*. Vishnu Sharma says that when we are in doubt as to what way should be followed in a particular situation, and the *Dharmasastra* points to the one way and the *Arthasastra* points to another, and there is a conflict between the two, we should follow the way of the Dharma and not the way of the Artha or worldly wisdom. Regarding morals, the work says that man should not be double-minded. In peculiar cases fraud could be practiced on one's enemies. Some people are of the opinion that fraud or pride (*dambha*) will ultimately be detected but Vishnu Sharma confides: 'Even Brahma cannot fathom a fraud cleverly devised.' And he also advises to be wise: "An enemy, although weak (possessed of little strength) if neglected by men blinded with pride through the fault of carelessness, then he, although manageable at first, becomes difficult to be subdued afterwards like a disease, which, though slight at first and easily curable, reaches the incurable stage if neglected in the beginning.'

Mitrabhedam, the first section (*tantra*) of the *Panchatantra*, shows how a great friendship that was growing between a lion, Pingalaka and a noble bull, Sanjeevaka was destroyed by a wicked and exceedingly ambitious jackal. Karataka. In it, the two jackal ministers, Karataka and Damanaka have narrated all the interwoven stories to the lion to persuade him to kill the bull. Of them, the 'Monkey and the Wedge' has been narrated to show that one should not poke one's nose in others' affairs: 'A man who wishes to meddle in affairs with which he is not concerned (which are no business of his) meets with destruction like the ape that pulled out the wedge.

The story of the 'Lion and the Rabbit' has been narrated to show the shrewdness and wit of the rabbit. The fable of the 'Swans and the Tortoise' has been told to prove the maxim that one should take advice from one's close friends and act accordingly and the fable of the 'Three Fishes' has suggested that one should be precautious and have an eye for the future. Only this section contains a large number of stories.

Mitrasampraktikam, the second *tantra* of the work shows the benefits of friendship. It tells us that wise men, gifted with genius and who are well informed, accomplish their purposes quickly, even without means, like the crow, the mouse, the deer and the tortoise. It discusses at length how even the weak are capable of saving themselves against their powerful enemies through mutual help. It illustrates the maxim, 'A friend in need is a friend indeed,' and narrates the frame-story of Hiranyaka, the mouse. The story of Manthara, the tortoise and Chitrangada, the deer show how the deer is saved by the united efforts of his friends as is said. 'He, who gains friends in this world and does not act crookedly towards them, does not, under any circumstances, suffer the pain of humiliation (or defeat).'

Kakolookeeyam, the third *tantra* of the work describes the enmity or war between crows and owls narrating: 'One should not trust a person once made hostile nor an enemy who has become a friend: see the cave that was full of owls was burnt down by the fire set by crows'. The frame story tells us that the King Arimariana seeks the advice of his four ministers regarding the captive Sthirajivan. But the ministers instead of giving advice give lectures on the excellence of kindness, treachery, bribing and of the employment of force respectively. Thus the advice has double meaning. 'The Ass in the Lion's Skin' and the 'Hare and the Tortoise' are the interesting stories. It is here that we come across the traditional teachings of the great Nitisastra writers like Brihaspati: 'Paropkarah punyay papaya parpeedanam.' Translated: Doing good to other leads to merit; giving trouble to others, to sin.

The *Labdhapranasham*, the fourth *tantra* of the work, narrates the story of the 'Monkey and the Crocodile' in which the monkey saves his life from the dangerous crocodile. The *Apareekashitakarakam*, the fifth *tantra* of the work, admonishes: 'A man should not act upon what he has imperfectly seen or known or heard or examined, as was done by a barber....'

Aesop's Fables, like the *Panchatantra*, also leave a lasting imprint of the imaginary and exciting world on the reader's mind. Though Aesop was a Greek slave, this master storyteller enthralled his readers about 600 B.C. Each of his stories, more aptly called a fable, has birds and animals as its main characters, which act and behave like human beings and illustrate success, or failure in a humorous way. In the end, there is a useful advice in the form of a moral. As we see in the fables of 'Wolf', 'The Monkey and the Fishermen', 'The Dog in the Manger', 'The Goose that Laid the Golden Eggs', etc.

Aesop introduces a number of animals such as ass, bull, camel, cat, crow, dog, fox, goose, hare, horse, hen, lion, mouse, monkey, owl, serpent, swan, tortoise, wolf, etc. He introduces his characters (animals) by their species as the Ass, the Lion and the Monkey and people introduced here are known by their professions such as carpenters, masons, merchants, millers, physicians, hunters, fishermen, cobblers, etc. The advantage of this method is that as soon as the name of the character is read or heard, the general behaviour of the species or people is brought to us immediately. They are categories, not individuals.

The are all occupied with one short narrative. For example, the three sentences in the fable 'The *Goose that laid the Golden Eggs'* set the stage: 'A cottager and his wife had a hen, which laid everyday a golden egg.' The second sentence tells what the man and his wife did: 'They supposed it must be containing a great lump of gold inside and killed it in order that they might get it, when to their surprise, they found that the hen differed in no respect from the other hens.' The third one tells the result: 'The foolish pair thus hoping to become rich all at once, were deprived of the gain of which they were assured day by day.' Every child may understand this vivid story and the strongest admonition against the greed that it gives. In spite of the brevity, the fable reveals human life by a sensitive and tender scrutiny.

Many of the fables are not the immediate work of Aesop: yet they bear the name of Aesop because he composed so large a number as to secure himself the right to be considered the father of the Greek fables. He is so far advanced before every competitor that all fables of this type and character are called Aesopic. The fable 'Hawk and the Nightingale' by Hesiod, 'The Fox Avenging his Wrongs on the Eagle' by Aeschylops and the 'Horse and the Stag' narrated by Aristotle at length are prior to the time of Aesop.

The Fables of Aesop emphasize the social interaction of human beings and the moral they draw tend to embody advice about the best way to deal with the competitive realities of life. Sometimes they do not teach moral lesson at all but constitute merely counsel of prudence and worldly wisdom based on peoples' observation of behaviour. Thus, in the fable 'Bat and the Weasel', the bat escaped death at the hands of the weasel once by claiming to be a bird and then by claiming to be an animal: 'I am not a mouse, I am a bird as you may see by my wings'. The weasel was compelled to acknowledge that mice have no wings and the cunning bat once more escaped death. Here the bat had spoken the truth in both the cases as the bat is neither a mouse nor a bird. There is no moral content. It only creates a laugh yet under a merry disguise to convey instruction. Self preservation is the centre of all the stories. The moral generalization is true with the story and cannot be separated from it. It appears that the moral content of the fable does not obtrude the story. But it is an inherent part of the action. We value it as an enrichment of the story.

The Aristotalian principles are represented in the Aesopian fables in miniature. As we see in the fable of the *'Maid and Her Servants'* where the action of the plot is confined within twenty-four hours and it takes place in only one place, in the house of the old lady: 'A certain old lady had several maids whom she used to call up to their work every morning at the crowing of the cock. Then the women who found it grievous to have their sweet sleep disturbed so early, combined together and killed the cock; thinking that, when the alarm was gone, they might enjoy themselves in their warm beds a little longer.

The old lady grieved at the loss of her cock, discovered the whole plot, was resolved to be even with them; for whom that moment she obliged them to rise constantly at midnight. 'The poor maids! Instead of getting more sleep, they found that with the cock gone, they hardly got any sleep at all.' The moral that springs from this fable is that you cannot outwit the crooked as also that the cunning meet their match.

Most of the fables in Aesop end with the remark of the principal character. They may simply be his last words as in the fable of the 'Monkey and the Fisherman'. A monkey perched upon a lofty tree saw some fishermen casting their nets into a river, and narrowly watched their proceedings. The fishermen after a while gave over fishing, and, on going home to dinner, left their nets upon the bank. The monkey, who is the most imitative of animals descended from the treetop, and endeavoured to do as they had done. Having handled the net he drew it into the river, but became engaged in the mesh. When drowning, he said to himself, 'I am rightly served; for what business had I who had never handled a net to try and catch fish?'

Extraordinary insight and sagacity are the salient features of the Fables of Aesop. They are loaded with the ripest wisdom of experience. A theme that appears again and again in the Aesopian Fables like the *Panchatantra* is that of the weak and insignificant somehow getting the better of the strong and the confident just as the little fishes were in the end luckier than the great fishes. The 'tortoise' manages to get the better of the 'hare' in the race. The 'mouse' too proves his worth to the mighty 'lion' when he gnaws through the ropes of the net in which the lion is trapped.

Another theme that appears again and again in the Aesopian fables like the *Panchatantra* is that of friendship. The fables of the 'Ass and its Purchaser' and the 'Goose and the Cranes' instruct us to make good companions and friends for one is known by the company he keeps. A purchaser wanted to purchase an ass and took one for a trial, and as soon as it went to the strawyard, it joined at once with the idlest and the greatest eater of them all. He thought to himself that this ass must also be of the same kind and led him back to his owner.

Both the works the *Panchatantra* and the *Aesop's Fables* aim at teaching worldly wisdom. The tales glorify the 'clever' animals, which survivc by outwitting there enemies. The *Panchatantra* tells us at the beginning of the book that the main purpose is to teach the princes the *rajniti* while *Aesop's Fables* do not have such aim. But there are fables like the 'Cat and the Cock,' 'The Wolf and the Lamb', 'The Lion and the Beasts', 'The Fowler and the Blackbird' etc., which warn us against tyrants and dictators.

The construction of the fable in both the works is very simple and direct. The most important is its terseness and epigrammatic force. For example, the fable 'Shepherd's Boy' contains only four sentences. The first one sets the stage: 'A certain shepherd's boy kept upon a common, and in sport and wantonness would often cry out 'The wolf! the wolf!' The second sentence tells what the people did: 'By this means he several times drew the husbandmen in an adjoining field from their work; who, finding themselves deluded resolved for the future to take no notice of his alarm.' The third one tells the result of his mischief: 'Soon after, the wolf came indeed. The boy cried out in earnest, but no heed being given to his cries, the sheep were devoured by the wolf.' This is the most popular story among the children that leaves a lasting impression on their mind with this moral: 'If faith is lost, everything is lost.'

In the *Panchatantra* the fables begin and end by a verse, which sums up the general maxim. 'Frequently, verses are embedded in Sanskrit prose works. In popular works such as the *Panchatantra* and the *Hitopadesa* verses are used in order to sum up in brief or in striking manner the moral of the preceding tale. The most striking feature of the work is that the fables in it are joined by means of boxed structure. It seems that the boxed structure originated to sustain interest in story-telling. It also indicates that the stories were narrated orally. It serves also as a link between the preceding and the next tale. But this is never found in Aesop, for he never tried to do so.

In the *Panchatantra*, a number of verses have been introduced that are all taken from the great epics like the *Mahabharata* and the *Ramayana* in order to justify the statements made by the characters. But Aesop has neither introduced such verses nor referred to his predecessors for the justification of the statements. Another characteristic difference between the *Panchatantra* and *Aesop's Fables* is that in the *Panchatantra*, the stories are told both in prose and verse. The verse is used for quoting the general maxim and the prose for narrating the fable. But in Aesop, we find only prose that is used for narrating the stories. In the *Panchatantra*, we come across a number of doctrines such as that of Jainism, Buddhism and Veerashaivism. There are a number of references to gods and faiths. Among them, the story of Devasharma throws light on Shaivism. But in Aesop, we do not come across any doctrine except some gods and angels as 'The Bees and the Jupiter', 'The Cat and the Venus', and 'The Crow and the Hercules'.

The *Panchatantra* is mainly based on the Karma theory. The earth where we are born is called the Karmabhumi. 'Lo! The food obtained at meal-time through the working of fate (luckily) cannot enter the mouth by any means without the exertion of the hand (unless the hand is used.)' The Karma law is a moral law. Vishnu Sharma teaches that good actions take us after our death to heaven and before our death bring us pleasure and happiness, and that bad actions bring unhappiness in this world and take us to hell after our death. 'Just as a calf finds out its mother even from the midst of thousands of cows, so the action done in a previous life follows its author (doer).' All our worldly wisdom is subject to this inevitable moral law of Karma. A good illustration of this is the incident in the story of Chitragreeva in *Mitrasampraktikam*, where Chitragreeva and its flock of followers are caught in a hunter's net and they go to Hiranyaka, Chitragreeva's mouse-friend. They ask it to cut the net with its teeth and free them. Hiranyaka proceeds to cut that part of the net, which is holding the king Chitragreeva. But the king says that the Hiranyak should cut that part of the net, which is holding servants. Now this may be against worldly wisdom but is deeply moral.

Vishnu Sharma does not believe in world brotherhood. One should first of all care for one's safety and then for the safety of others. This world may have some friends for us but mostly has indifferent people and enemies. So Hiranyaka reminds Chitragreeva of worldly wisdom and that self-preservation is the first duty of the master and that the safety of the servants comes only in the second place. Vishnu Sharma believed in the Karma theory: most of his fables are only illustrations in defence of it. It is because of this theory that the work is read and enjoyed even today. But in Aesop we do not find any such Karma theory. The *Panchatantra* has this element rather than the virtue. Thus the animal tale retains its original landscape of 'nature red in tooth and claw.' It is a cruel competitive world in which creatures live by their cleverness and take the advantage of the foolishness of others. This picture and world-view are still retained by the animal tale.

An outstanding feature of the animal and bird characters in the *Panchatantra* is that they are all given their meaningful names, thus the lion is Madotkata, the merchant is Jeernadhana, a fish is Anagatavidhata. In Aesop they are known by their species. In both the works, the characters behave like human beings. We forget for a moment that they are animals and birds in the garb of human beings.

A story of the *Panchatantra* that attracts the reader most and also gives a lesson, tells that a true friend may not be able to help a person because of person's own stupidity. This is well exemplified in the fable of 'Shell-Neck, Slim and Grim'. The two cranes decide to take a tortoise from a dead lake to another more pleasant one, as an act of friendship. They hold a stick in between their beaks and the tortoise hangs to the stick holding it in its mouth. The tortoise is amazed by the beauty of the aerial landscape and forgets what the cranes told it — 'Be careful, Be careful. Do not open your mouth in the sky. You'll see all kinds of wonderful things down below, but never open your mouth in wonder. 'If you will do, you'll fall. You have to keep your mouth tightly shut. I certainly will,' said the tortoise. The moment it exclaims something, it slips down to the ground and is smashed to jelly. It must be noted here that the cranes belong to the air, the turtle to the earth. Even a temporary flight makes the turtle giddy with intoxication. And the good intentions of the cranes have come to naught, because they contravened the nature of the turtle. The aim of the fable is that even friends cannot help a fool. But here the foolish tortoise assumes a quality more than that of a confirmed fool like a donkey.

Another fable that attracts the child and lives in mind for its own sake, without any reference to its moral significance, is the 'Dog in the Manger.' A dog lay in a manger, and by his growling and snapping prevented the oxen from eating the hay which had been placed for them. 'What a selfish Dog!' said one of them to his companions, 'He cannot eat the hay himself and yet refuses to allow those to eat who can.' Every child knows this vivid story.

Humanization of animals through the social relationship is a more dominant impulse. The lion, for example, the king of the forest, reflects a human quality. Modern cartoonists follow this process of ascribing human qualities to animals. The cartoons in newspaper caricature human behaviour often presenting animals in anthropomorphized form. When animals talk like men, we at least feel as if we were listening to old men like children.

The intention in making use of animals and birds as characters seems to be that the reader perceives the similarity between himself and the actor in the fable. And hence the conclusion that her/his actions will lead to the same consequences as of the animal or bird in the fable. The reader always identifies with the characters and enjoys or suffers with them. It must be noted that the lower animals think and act like human beings, and it is for this reason that modern psychologists study animal's behaviour in the hope that it would throw light on the fundamental principles of human behaviour.

'Man now lives in a very practical and matter-of-fact age, and his daily drudgery and monotonous life cannot satisfy the craving for romance that is more or less universal in human beings. So he seeks romance in fables and the grown-up as well as children read the fables. Though he knows very well that fables are fiction, he finds pleasure in reading them because they take him away for a little time from his dull and monotonous life. Moreover, fables are good for children because they express and keep alive the sense of wonder.' La Fontaine remarks, 'Plato...gave Aesop a place of honour, hoping that the young would absorb fables along with their mother's milk.' Locke recommends fables in teaching children and refers to *Aesop's Fables* as 'the only book almost I know fit for children.' As it appeals to the sense of fun, Joseph Addison is right when he says, 'Fables were the first pieces of wit that made their appearance in the world and have been still highly valued not only in times of the greatest simplicity but among the most polite ages of mankind.' There are no regions of experience or speculation into which the fables do not penetrate and gather sustenance for the imagination.

'Some books are to be tasted, others to be swallowed and some few to be chewed and digested,' observes Lord Francis Bacon. The fables in the *Panchatantra* and Aesop's are to be chewed and digested. Both of these works have stood the test of time and have been read, recited and enjoyed by readers all over the world. The animal fable right from the *Panchatantra* and the *Aesop's Fables* to the comics of Walt Disney and Hannah Barbera are closely associated with a moral lesson, which usually governs its end as a generalization for which the story is the example. *The Panchatantra*, 'may be considered as a mirror, reflecting light friendly to other sciences, and facilitating to those, who are acquainted with its contents, the acquirement of worldly wisdom' — Vishnu Sharma. Thus, the fable that takes the readers away from this fretful and noisy world for a little time and influences their mind wholly, makes them fit and learn all that is essential for performing duties and developing qualities.

References

The Folk-Tale. 1946. New York: Holt, Rinehart and Winston.

Pawate, C.I. 1986. *The Panchatantra and Aesop's Fables*. Delhi: Amar Prakashan.

International Dictionary of Thoughts. 1969. Chicago: J.G. Ferguson and Company.

Kale, M.R. ed. and trans. 1912. *Panchatantra of Vishnu Sharma*. Delhi: Motilal Banarsidas. Reprint, 1999.

Indian Fairy Tales. 1959. New York: Criterion Books.

The *Panchatantra and the Hitopadesa Stories*. 2000. Mumbai: Taraporewale and Sons Ltd.

New Gul Mohar Graded English Course, Reader 5. 2000. Hyderabad: Oriental Longman.

The Fables of La Fontaine. 1954. Trans. by Mariane Moore. New York: The Viking Press.

Gay, Pater John. 1964. *Locke on Education*. New York: Routledge.

Bond, Donald, K. 1970. *Critical Essays from the Spectator*. London: The Clarendon Press.

Bacon, Francis. 1968. *Essays*. London: J.M. Dent. and Sons.

10

An Analysis of the Relationship between Children and Adults in Three Indian English Novels

Marina Goglio

Novels dealing with children usually narrate how the young protagonists learn to cope with the troubles involved in the process of growth and in their relationship with adults. The journey that leads children towards adolescence and maturity, towards the comprehension of adult rules. Roles have been defined by Hariprasanna as 'a progress from innocence to experience, from innocent pleasures of childhood to youth and to maturity' (25). The first attempts of children into such an intricate world usually cause misunderstandings and states of confusion both for children and adults. This is the case of the absent-minded and innocent Swaminathan in *Swamy and Friends* by R.K. Narayan (1935), of the egocentric and ambitious Mulky in *Pilpali Sahab* by M.R. Anand (1990) and of the introvert and silent Jehangir in *Tales From Firozsha Baag* by Rohinton Mistry (1987).

In the idyllic and imagined city of Malgudi, the ten years old Swaminathan lives his everyday struggle against school friends and family. In particular, he is in constant and conflicting relationship with the agents of power embodied by male authorities: father, teachers and headmasters, deceiving coachmen, doctors and forest officers. They force him to rebellion against the oppressive regime of adults. His acts of defiance towards authority partake basically of a twofold nature: a passive resistance that ends in the two hurried escapes from the two schools and an active one results in acts of violence, such as the throwing of stones at the windows of the school or the burning of his school cap when he joins a demonstration against the English Government in India. Not only are adults depicted as unsympathetic agents of power, but they even turn out to be untrustworthy and prone to deceive young and innocent children. Swaminathan lays bare his simple-mindedness when he is induced by a coachman to give him six pies, in order to multiply them by means of magic ritual, 'He wanted only six pies to start with; in a short time he would make it six annas, and after that convert it to six rupees' (Narayan: 68). The same episode occurs in the Italian romance *Pinocchio* by Collodi (1883) when the credulous puppet Pinocchio is deceived by the Cat and the Fox, and persuaded to bury his money in the Field of Miracles for multiplication.

Swamy and Friends reaches its climax when Swaminathan is about to be punished by the headmaster of the Board School, for not participating in the Drill and Scouting classes, "The Head Master held the cane ready and cried: 'Hold out your hand, six on each hand for each day of absence, and the whole of the next lesson on the bench. [...] if you miss a single class again, I shall strip you in the school hall and ask the peon to cane you.' (Narayan: 144). Indeed, school is the first place where children have to confront with adults without any protection by their families. Consequently they have to learn how to relate with teachers and headmasters and other agents of power. As Swaminathan has already escaped from the Albert Mission School for a similar reason, we should view the episode in the light of a critical act of self-awareness against the adult world, given that the character speaks of himself as 'the enemy of the school' (Narayan: 146).

Like Peter Pan in J.M. Barrie's novel (1911), he too feels the oppression of the future and decides to abandon the world of Malgudi. Rejecting the dictatorship of Time he refuses to grow and he is ready to abandon his family, his friends and his city to live outside society, as the newborn Peter Pan did. The rebel Swaminathan refuses the domineering power exercised by the headmaster of the Board School, who is going to cane him. As a reactive response to the injustice implied in this imposition of discipline, the boy throws the cane out of the window and leaves the institute. Having defied the rules, he must be considered an outlaw. Free from any bond and schedule he starts wandering in the city, until he reaches the school from which he has been excluded, exactly as Pater Pan has been shut out of his own house by a barred window. 'Long ago,' he said, 'I thought like you that my mother would always keep the window open for me; so I stayed away for moons and moons and moons, and then flew back; but the window was barred, for mother had forgotten all about me, and there was another little boy sleeping in my bed' (Barrie: 139).

The exclusion of Swaminathan, shut out by a gate from his previous school, makes him desirous of being part again of the daily activities of that place. Being a Peter Pan-like figure, an outcast, he can exercise a charming attraction towards children. When he is staring longingly towards the school he sees a boy and calls him, 'The small person took just a second to decide whether to obey the call of that apparition or to run back to the class. Swaminathan called him again. And the very small man drew towards him as if in a hypnotic state, staring wildly' (Narayan: 147).

His journey towards Neverland, that is intended to free Swaminathan from the impositions of Time, is interrupted when he enters the Mempi Forest, a Dantesque—like 'dark forest' symbolizing the protagonist's puzzlement and his struggle against his fears. The forest, a place that represents the confusing age that ushers in adolescence, also stands for the necessity of coming to terms with the rules of adult life and also constitutes the place for a rite of passage, in which the boy is forced to recognize his mistakes and his fears in coping with authority. Like a neophyte who is unable to face the difficulties of a new formative experience he needs a guide and, indeed, when he is about to succumb he is finally rescued by an adult, the Forest Officer. His *guru*-rescuer carries him to a place in which it seems possible to stop Time or where, at least, Time seems not to matter, almost as it were a transposition of the literary Neverland of Barrie,

> 'What day is this, sir?'.
>
> ...'This is Sunday'.
>
> 'What? What?' Swaminathan stood petrified. Sunday! He gazed dully at the heap of stones at his feet.
>
> 'What is the matter?'
>
> 'The match is on Sunday', Swaminathan stammered.
>
> 'What if it is? You have still a day before you. This is only Saturday' (Narayan: 165)

Thus reassured by the man who rescued him when he was lost in confusion, Swaminathan has to face a further betrayal, when he discovers that the Forest Officer has deceived him, as the actual day is Sunday and not Saturday and so he has missed the cricket match. His attempt to abandon Malgudi and to become a Peter Pan-like figure is thus thwarted and the boy has to accept his own role inside society. But, definitely, in this novel, 'innocence is precarious and threatened' (Ram: 3) by experience such as embodied in deceiving adults.

Communication between children and adults is to be considered a Utopia; in this perspective are noteworthy the episodes concerning the exchange of letters between the boys and the dealer in sports articles and the mathematical problem Swaminathan's father imposes on him to solve. Commercial letters are exchanged between the newborn cricket team of M.C.C. and Messrs Binns' shop of sport goods, in which children use a direct approach and ask, with extrovert impudence, to be sent the equipment for their team even if they are not, at the moment, able to pay for it. Messrs Binns' answer is so full of business terms so as to puzzle Swaminathan and his friends, who think that the letter is not for them. The second episode occurs when the father of the protagonist, who is on vacation, asks his son to solve a problem dealing with ten mangoes sold at fifteen rupees all together (Narayan: 86).

Although he only has to apply the proportion's rules, Swaminathan feels rather uncomfortable, as he does not know whether the mangoes could or could not be ripe, given that to ask fifteen rupees for unripe fruit would be unfair. So, whereas Swaminathan is worried about the ripeness of mangoes and its relation with the price of the fruit, his father is simply asking him to think in mathematical terms. In this novel, adults and children live in different dimensions and communication between the two worlds seems to be almost impossible, every attempt causing misunderstandings, betrayals or failures. Swaminathan's response and ultimate solution to adult intrusiveness is to posit an implied way of escape.

Young Mulky in *Pilpali Sahab* lives with his family at the periphery of an English military cantonment, admiring the English officers who behave self-confidently and are well aware of their right to be respected and even feared by their subordinates. His approach towards the structures of power, again represented by male characters, is different from Swaminathan's. Being younger than the other children he is almost always alone and he cannot rely on a supportive group of friends, so that his response to the punishments meted out by his teachers and to the harassment of adults deploys a strong desire to acquire the same authoritative power that he perceives in the Englishmen, so as to be respected and obeyed as they are. In particular, he relates authority to the 'Angrezi Sahabs' and starts nurturing a desire to be himself a *sahab* too, thinking *sahabness* could be a feature one can acquire by means of money or by means of good school marks. Wondering about the way he can become an Englishman, he is aware of his brown skin and elaborates strategies to whiten his face although, 'the more I thought about this aspiration, the more I realized that only by acquiring a hat of one kind or another, either a helmet as a gift from some Tommy, or a peak cap from the shop of a Kabaria rag shop, or the *sola topee* in the Quarter Guard, could I become a sahab' (Anand: 8). The 'sola topee', a typical colonial hat, is thus attributed the power to irradiate 'Englishness' on its owner and raise him to the status of a *sahab*. That is what young Mulky believes and what

Surjan Singh tells him when he presents the boy with the English hat, 'He took the sola topee off the peg and put it on my head. It was far too large. He smiled and said good humouredly: 'Go now, you are a Sahab!' (Anand: 83).

In *The Interpretation of Dreams* by Freud (1900) hats are described as symbols of masculinity, and in particular as a representation of the male genitals 'Of articles of dress, a woman's hat may very often be interpreted with certainty as the male genitals' (Freud, chapter 6. 'The Dream-Work', 'E. Representation in Dreams by Symbols: Some further Typical Dreams'). So the strong desire felt by Mulky to possess a hat, and in particular, either a 'helmet' or a 'sola topee' (the former being associated with military uniform, the latter a universal symbol of colonial power and authority), is the manifestation of the fact that Mulky is associating authority and its paraphermalia to Englishmen and to adults in general. This very connection relating a hat and adult power is described in *Swamy and Friends* too. The young protagonist is developing a rebellious attitude towards authority, and when dragged into a Gandhian boycott strike he burns his cap, 'Somebody asked him: "Young man, do you want our country to remain in eternal slavery?" Swaminathan quailed with shame, "Oh, I didn't notice," he said and removing his cap flung it into the fire with a feeling that he was saving the country' (Narayan: 95).

The relationship between Mulky and power is jeopardized by the frequent moves and journeys of his family, whose mobility confronts him with rather different realities, as for instance the hierarchy-ordered military cantonment, the noisy and multicoloured coppersmith quarter in Amritsar, the rude and conservative rural village of Daska. Whenever he spends some days in a different place he develops a fondness for different people and starts wishing to be himself a different person. For instance, when he is in the Nowshera cantonment his heroes are the 'Angrezi Sahabs' but rather incongruously when in Daska, his maternal village, he develops a strong desire to be like the young prince Daleep Singh that fought against the English Army to free his kingdom.

Indeed, his thinking as a boy is incoherent as, for instance, he pesters his parents to be sent to school like the elder boys, even if he is too young to be admitted. When he finally succeeds in convincing his parents his first encounter with power terrifies him to such a degree as to make him refuse any further contact with didactic methods, "Master Din Gul [...] got up cane in hand, went near the boys who were holding ears and struck all of them one blow each, shouting: 'Bottoms up!' Two of the boys began to sob. I had tears in my eyes. [...] I began to cry and fell in a heap rolling on the ground. [...] When I faced father, I said: 'I don't want to go to school again...' And I began to sob. 'One day I will also be asked to hold ears' by Master Din Gul,' I said! 'So I don't want to go to school" (Anand: 61-63). Mulky is thus forced to recognize the oppressiveness of adults and even to share the conclusion reached by Swaminathan about them: they deceive children, 'And I felt all elders lied to children' (Anand: 68).

In 'The Collector' from *Tales From Firozsha Baag*, the author focuses on a relationship between an adult and an adolescent, one initially grounded on mutual respect and comprehension, but finally doomed to indifference and oblivion on the part of the boy. Jehangir too, like Mulky, is excluded from the other children's plays and he develops an attachment for Dr. Mody that, attracted by the boys shyness and politeness, invites him to be his disciple in a sort of *guru-chela*, or *senex-puer*, relationship. The boy is invited to see the stamp-collection of Dr. Mody and to share his interest in the hoarding of valuable, exotic or just charming stamps. The desire of Dr. Mody to be the wise *guru* who guides a young neophyte towards knowledge is frustrated by his son preferring rather different activities, 'Fate denied fruition to all of Dr. Mody's plans; and when he talked about stamps, Pesi laughed and mocked his beloved hobby' (Mistry: 82). Jehangir is thus the substitute *puer* that the *senex-guru* Dr. Mody chooses as his chela. The *guru* discloses for the *chela*, literally, the doors of a cupboard full of stamps to be collected in the stamp albums, 'But Burjor Uncle led him instead to a cupboard in the corner in the room. [...] Each of the cupboard's four shelves was piled with biscuit tins and sweet tins [...] Burjor Uncle reached out for a box at random and showed him inside. It was chock-full of stamps!' (Mistry: 88), and consequently starts a series of meetings that acquire the significance of an esoteric ritual' (Mistry: 95). Jehangir, charmed by the treasure cupboard and magic rituals, is thus dazzled and attracted by Dr. Mody, but his apprenticeship will soon be abruptly interrupted, because of the disappearance of the Spanish dancing-lady stamp, the most valuable piece in the collection.

Three years later, after Dr. Mody's death, Jehangir is asked to accept his guru's inheritance, his stamp collecton. Unable and unwilling to be the heir of Dr. Mody, the boy locks all the stamps in an old trunk, and when he finally decides to think as to what to do with the collection and opens again the trunk he finds that an army of cockroaches and white ants has destroyed it, sealing the conclusion, and failure, of his apprenticeship period.

Thus the process of growth, laden with manifold discoveries and acts of coming to terms, is traced in the works analysed in my paper, from the first conscious acts of the four years old Mulky to the almost sixteen Jehangir. The end of childhood is represented by a strong image of destruction: the insects that infest and devour the memories and evidences of the past. A similar act of destruction is described in the poem by E. Birney 'First Tree for Frost' collected in *Poesie* (1991) in which a child, instructed by his father, waters the spruce tree that should grow together with the boy. During the cold Canadian winter he tries to warm the tree by watering it with his urine, thus dooming it to death. So the growth of the child is associated with the failure of his relationship with Nature, although such a failure encloses a necessary step towards experience and maturity. In a similar way, Jehangir's ripening of age evokes the interfacing, and apparently cruel image of the cockroaches and white ants that destroy pitilessly the heritage that the *senex* left as his unique legacy to the *purer*. Growing of age may be a sad and harsh process, one implying separation and forgetfulness.

References

Narayan, R.K. 1935. *Swamy and Friends*. Madras: Indian Thought Publications. Reprint, 1999.

Anand, Mulkraj. 1990. *Pilpali Sahab. The Story of a Big Ego in a Small Body*. New Delhi: Arnold Publishers.

Mistry, R.1987: *Tales from Firozsha Baag*. Markham: Penguin Books.

Barrie, J.M. 1911. *Peter Pan*. Harmondsworth: Penguin Books. Reprint, 1976.

Collodi, C. 1983. *The Adventures of Pinoùhio: Story of a Puppet*. Berkeley: University of California Press. Reprint, 1886.

Hariprasana, A. 1994. *The World of Malgudi. A Study of R.K. Narayan's Novels*. New Delhi: Prestige.

Ram, A. 1981. *Perspectives on R.K. Narayan*, Ghaziabad, Vimal Prakashan. Freud, Sigmund. *The Interpretation of Dreams*, first English edition published by Macmillan, New York, in 1913 (1900). E-text available on: http://psychclassics,yorku,ca/Freud/ Dreams.

Birney, E. 1991. *Poesie*. Rome: Bulzoni. (bilingual edition).

Note

A romance for children is that that narrates the adventures of a wooden puppet who is idle, credulous and an impenitent liar. His main desire is to become a real body, but before this could happen he has to learn to be human, *i.e.* generous and unselfish.

11

Harry Potter and the Magic of Growing up through Fiction

Esterino Adami

The ground-breaking novels of Joanne K. Rowling have brought to light the significance of children's literature and the salient position of adolescent characters. In their enormous popularity, these texts try to detect the intricate relationship between the process of growing and the handling of fantasy. In various times and ways, children in literature express plenty of values and their stories are dramatised through the modes of folk-tale and romance, rather than following the style of social realism. Harry Potter, Pinocchio, Peter Pan, Dorothy witness generational transformations in a constructive manner as fables and fantastic adventures stimulate both children and adults. They incorporate moral or ethic values, in inexplicit forms that have to be decoded and, while providing a reassuring distinction between good and evil, they refer not to the 'real' life, but to inner processes of growing and living by means of metaphors and clichés. Reading these fairy tales, which are constructed as prototypes, may be a sort of therapy that young people employ to investigate into or soothe their directionless confusion.

The Harry Potter novels, published between 1997 and 2003, include *Harry Potter and the Philosophical Stone*, *Harry Potter and the Chamber of Secrets*, *Harry Potter and the*

Prisoner of Azkaban, *Harry Potter and the Goblet of Fire* and the very recent *Harry Potter and the Order of the Phoenix*. Although these texts are located under the generic and imprecise critical umbrella of children's literature, as a whole they build a complex thematic texture. Given such intermingled composition, I shall concentrate upon the first volume, which inaugurated the series, in order to spotlight some central motifs.

By drawing on sources galore, Rowling writes a story that is both simple and complex: young Harry Potter, who initially lives a Cinderella-like condition, is then invited to join Hogwarts, the school of magicians. In its linearity, the plot is deftly decorated by colourful details and rich imagery. It pictures a rite of passage from one age to another and examines some fundamental issues of childhood: the idea of family, friendship and personal identity. The two paradigms that govern the entire narrative structure of the Scottish novelist are the never-ending clash between the Manichean forces of good and evil, and the image of Hogwarts as a mirror of school systems, with particular reference to British 'public schools' and colleges.

Notably, Harry from his birth bears a scar on his forehead, which is a sign left by the dark lord Voldemort, whose name frightens and is always omitted, and this stands as a symbol of doubleness, a combination of positive and negative elements. In his unsophisticated and dialectical style, Hagrid the Keeper of the Keys who helps the boy to reach the land of magicians, reveals some hidden secrets. Being a sort of putative father, he admonishes Harry and supplies some more fragments concerning the death of his parents:

> 'You-Know-Who killed 'em. An' then—and this is the real myst'ry of the story—he tried to kill you, too. Wanted ter make a clean job of it, I suppose, or may be he just liked killin' by then. But he couldn't do it. Never wondered how you got that mark on yer forehead? That was no ordinary cut. That's what yeh get when a powerful, evil curse touches yeh—took care of yer mum an' dad an' yer house, even—but it didn't work on you, an' that's why yer

famous, Harry. No one ever lived after he decided ter kill 'em, no one except you, an' he'd killed some o' the best witches an' wizards of the age—the McKinnons, the Bones, the Prewtts—an' you was only a baby, an' you lived.' (*HPPS*: 45-46)

Hagrid's words have the purpose to advise and warn the magical adolescent so that he can act wisely and mitigate his emotive chaos, implied de facto in such a tumultuous phase of his life. By providing some insights into Harry's story, the clumsy and gentle half-giant wishes to express the dichotomy of values shared by the young: only if he can comprehend his contradictions (his idiosyncratic doubleness) and his nebulous impulses, the protagonist will be able to progress and deal with the intricacies of life. Indeed, Harry who experiences the anxieties and doubts of adolescence has to quest himself in order to calibrate his decisions and actions. However, his destiny is lucidly designated in a kind of premonition, so that he acquires the essence of 'an Arthurian hero: the boy who can pull the sword from the stone and who has a role to play in shaping the future of the world' (Eccleshare: 17).

In the text, we find numerous instances of contrasting images, such as the rivalry between the school houses of Gryffindor and Slytherin, or the shabby pseudo-familiar milieu dominated by Uncle Vernon and Aunt Petunia versus the festive atmosphere of Hogwarts. Yet it is significant, from a psychological point of view, to observe that sometimes the contours of the frame of mind of the different characters are blurred or contradictory. Professor Snape, for instance, is an ambiguous figure: in his Potions lessons, he looks like a gothic character, often behaving roughly and playing the role of the villain. For some apparently unknown reasons (but the truth will be revealed in end), he loathes Harry Potter and this emerges in his teaching activity too, when he explains how to use powdered root of asphodel and the infusion of wormwood. However, during a match of Quidditch, the official sport of wizards astutely invented by Rowling, professor Snape silently protects the boy, whose flying broomstick has been bewitched by professor Raptor, and therefore turns out to have a positive function. In fact, in spite of his peaceful and stammering quiet voice, Raptor is the cruel servant of Voldemort and the real enemy of Harry. Rowling seems to suggest that the inversion of roles is symbolically evocative of oppositional forces and hidden truths. Harry is shown grand models of behaviour and must work out his own strategy of growing up. When Jung speaks of the notion of shadow, he describes the inner, unclear aspects of ego which may be rather problematic, though not necessarily negative or oppositional to conscious self. The shadow may feature creativity and imagination, two characteristics which are both needed by the individual. Harry perceives the type of mental confusion and the Sorting Hat, a magical speaking object that decides to which school house the new pupils will belong, confirms his perplexity.

Yet, as the story unfolds its subplots, Harry proves to be able to discern between different options and finally avoid grim and selfishness; in such manner, he embodies the symbolic struggle of personality integration against chaotic disintegration. Through the use of modern exemplar, the novel is grounded on the tenets of Bildungsroman, a typical genre within children's literature which charts the winding path of formation of the young personage. Furthermore the mode of fantastic literature allows the author to restore a tainted balance, and as a result, the happy ending becomes an encouraging message for children. Although the realms of fantasy and 'reality' are distinctively separated, the analytical construction of fables, which are peculiarly close to dreams, projects a gaze onto the unconscious and alludes to the dimension of the self.

However, Harry finds that scanning his own innermost thoughts and feelings can be a slippery operation. The boy, who bemoans the demise of his parents, experiences a 'truncated' existence since he is cleft from his real domestic identity, but he longs for a sense of completeness. When the protagonist evokes memories and dreams through the Mirror of Erised, the magical object works as an empty screen onto which one can project the self. The ghostly images of James and Lily Potter represent the boy's desires pictured in an illusionary palimpsest. Albus Dumbledore, the wise headmaster of Hogwarts, illustrates the miraculous virtue of the arcane mirror to the boy and in so doing he acts as a suitable tutor and therapist: [...] 'Now, can you think what the Mirror of Erised shows us all?'

Harry shook his head.

'Let me explain. The happiest man on earth would be able to use the Mirror of Erised like a normal mirror, that is, he would look into it and see himself exactly as he is. Does that help?'

Harry thought. Then he said slowly, 'It shows us what we want...whatever we want...'

'Yes and no,' said Dumbledore quietly. 'It shows us nothing more or less than the deepest, most desperate desire of our hearts. You, who have never known your family, see them standing around you. Ronald Weasley, who has always been overshadowed by his brothers, sees himself standing alone, the best of all of them. However this mirror will give us neither knowledge or truth. Men have wasted away before it, entranced by what they have seen, or being driven mad, not knowing if what it shows is real or even possible' (HPPS: 156-157).

What the adolescent character must learn is to acquire confidence in himself, because this is the only stratagem by which one can tackle difficulties and tensions. In Rowling's writing, magic serves as an instrument to highlight the faceted condition of children and youth in general. It is worth noticing that, frequently, in fables mirrors constitute a device that connects the Self with the Other, the insideness with the outsideness, the world of 'reality' and that of fancy. Lewis Carrol's *Through the Looking-Glass* (1872), for instance, expresses the subverting effect of going beyond borders: Alice reaches an alternative universe and her experiences thematise the efforts of growing and shifting from one psychological frame to another. The power of the mirror may be lethal, as the myth of Narcissus suggests, but in Rowling's text operates a cathartic disburdening, a self-confrontation to fortify one's personality.

Other magical devices relate the idea of a journey, or transformation or passage, to the experience of growing and changing, physically and mentally. In other words, they become rites of passage. The main entry point to Hogwarts is platform nine and three-quarters at King's Cross railway station in London and such precise topographical indication tries to anchor the narrative of wizards to the world of Muggles, a term the author mints to indicate people with no magical powers. Indeed, 'its public location, rather than the privacy of a domestic interior or point of access, makes it a more social and less personal fantasy at the outset' (Eccleshare: 65). On their way to the school of enchantments, the pupils need no flying carpets or magical lamps: they simply board the Hogwarts Express, a steam train of long-gone times. Later the dimension of the journey towards Hogwarts and the encounter with the world of sorcery assumes the form of a character-building practice and the children will be required to make their own decisions, to ponder and eventually discern good from evil.

Let us observe the main setting of Harry Potter's adventures: Hogwarts, a supernatural place, which is similar to a medieval castle and borrows some characteristics from British 'public schools'. In the context of traditional children's literature, the novel restores the scholarly atmosphere and dilates it into an educational laboratory at work, which is shaped through the sense of camaraderie, friendship or enmity, learning and belonging. Children severed from parental guidance make up groups or clans and, in thus doing, they construe a collective identity instead of a personal domain; further we should note that the relationship between them and their respective houses is profound and indicative of their qualities. The school, whose Victorian name evokes foggy stories of Dickensian memory, presents a cluster of towers, turrets, haunted halls, leaded windows, and ghosts. However the author updates and lampoons her gothic narrative in a modern pastiche, so that the fearful monster that guards the entry to the school's shelter of the philosophical stone, a three-headed huge dog that reminds one of Cerberus, the hellish creature of classic mythology, is given a very funny and harmless name: Fluffy. Rowling celebrates the scholarly ethos—the importance of education and its application to life—in various forms, in particular by virtue of the game of Quidditch, since sports serve the purpose to strengthen this type of cohesion. The writer is aware that children of all ages consider boarding schools a claustrophobic sites that dwindle their freedom, but she wittily manipulates characters and plots in a captivating fashion. Moreover, she subtly mocks the parochial rigidity of British private institutes. For instance, the letter inviting Harry to attend Hogwarts displays a miscellany of formality and fantasy; it reads:

Hogwarts School of Witchcraft and Wizardry

Headmaster: Albus Dumbledore (Order of Merlin, First Class, Grand Sore., Chf. Warlock.

Supreme Mugwump, International Confed. of Wizards)

Dear Harry Potter,

We are pleased to inform you that you have a place at Hogwarts School of Witchcraft and Wizardry. Please find enclosed a list of all necessary books and equipment.

Term begins on 1 September. We await your owl by no later than 31 July.

Yours Sincerely,

Minerva McGonagall

Deputy Headmistress (HPPS: 42-43)

Magical schools, with their hierarchies and rules, stage a social microcosm, so that different themes can be processed. In Rowling's text, Hogwarts gives birth to groups and genuine friendships; from a pedagogical point of view, this form of aggregation that Harry experiments, especially in relation with Ron and Hermione, is a sort of physiological need, whose function is different from that of the family. It also constitutes a social debut and creates strong bonds: the young hero and his two close companions make up a dynamic fellowship that suggests the notion of unity and allegiance, to the detriment of egoistic individualism. This is the proper spirit of being part of a house: Gryffindor therefore becomes Harry's re-invented home, a handsome reward that redeems the past vexation of Uncle Vernon and Aunt Petunia.

As Italian psychologist and psychotherapist Rita Ricci (53-61) holds, the notion of membership is pregnant in adolescence as it provides a reference system, and at Hogwarts each house functions as a 'social family', one in which the student is given a chance to build up interpersonal contacts and individual identity through confrontation, collaboration and the sharing of sundry experiences amongst peers. Characteristically, the school bears the Latin motto Draco Dormines Nunquam Titillandus while each house is illustrated in heraldic symbols: a serpent for Slytherins, an eagle for Ravenclaws, a badger for laborious Hufflepuff and a rampant lion for courageous Gryffindors. As I have already hinted at, the merits and attributes of the students are strictly connected with the values expressed by the school's animal imagery. Here the novelist points out the scholarly tradition of colleges and the role of animals in fables and storytelling. In a psychological interpretation, animals refer to id and allude to instinctive and animal nature of the individual, whereas on a literary terrain, they operate as the typical characters of children's fiction.

In such type of narratives, animals may be anthropomorphised figures, sometimes accompanied by other non-human creatures. Martin Hocke's trilogy, for example, is constructed as a saga of owls and their tribulations with dangerous mankind. Also here the building aspect, that concerns the process of formation and growth, is a primary motif. In *The Ancient Solitary Reign* (1989), the protagonist, an owl called Hunter, needs some tools of knowledge in order to deal with both owls and men. Hunter and his brother are looked after by their mother, Dapple:

'Who teaches us?' asked Hunter.

'I teach you,' Dapple said. 'I teach you the basic theory of everything except religion. Since your father is the Religion Owl on the Barn owl council, he is much better qualified to teach you that.'

'How many subjects are there?' Quaver asked.

'Eight, altogether,' said Dapple. 'History, geography, ecology, religion, human studies, and owlology. I've already told you...' 'What is owlology?' interrupted Hunter, who wished that Quaver and his mother would not tear away at things with such bewildering speed.

'Owlology is the study of owl behaviour patterns and philosophies,' said Dapple. 'Not only Barn owls, but all other species, too, especially our neighbours the Tawnies and the little immigrants, since with both of these we have to co-exist' (114-15).

In both Rowling and Hocke, subjects to learn and identities to be shaped are central themes and usually constitute a main frame within which subplots are expanded and parallel the maelstrom of growth. The Scottish author in particular focuses on the relevancy of the notion of learning, a process that encompasses both the cognitive powers of the boy's mind and his emotions and imagination, and broadly speaking all the reaches of the adolescent's personality. Harry progressively understands that the acquisition of knowledge signifies how to exploit opportunities and such tactic allows him to become master of his own fate. Implicitly, the psychological approach adopted by Rowling concerns the key performance of learning, which appeals to the highest and primordial aspects of the mind, entailing as it does id, ego and superego, especially in a period when the adolescent's basic personality is being formed. Harry's character and vision change systematically after his introduction to Hogwarts and the world of wizardry: there he eventually manages to 'put himself into actions' and become an active agent: therefore he develops a new identity and offsets the suffocating climate of his substitutive family in the land of Muggles, with the domineering figures of Uncle Vernon and Aunt Petunia.

Whether the scholarly population of Hogwarts metaphorically and metonymically represents society in generic terms, it is plausible for the novelist to inscribe contemporary topics like class and race: in fact 'wizard hierarchies are based on many things, including age, wealth and intelligence, but the central issue for the fanatics is one of purity of breeding.' (Eccleshare: 75). Such argument lies at the heart of the distinction of subcategories like 'pure blood', indicating the children from ancient families of magicians who have not been 'corrupted' by the external world, and 'mixed blood', with reference to those pupils whose parents may be Muggles, sometimes labelled as 'Mudbloods'. However the writer treats the core of hybridity as a constructive element in view of the fact that both Harry and Hermione have strong links with the Muggle world. To gain prestige and affirm their own identities, these characters have to develop their learning skills and practice them so that Harry, whose mother was not born into a magical family, and Hermione, a first-generation apprentice wizard whose parents are dentists in the external world, prove to be perfectly integrated into the universe of witchcraft and sorcery.

Such powerful metaphor of mongrelisation discards the falseness of purity and celebrates the resource of plurality and polyphony in a narrative strategy that is akin to the hotchpotch of cultures that preoccupies postcolonial literatures. In such mixed society and inclusive community imagined by the novelist, once again we observe how emphasis is laid upon the concept of qualification and education as means that the children need to act independently and achieve integration. Indeed, Ron too demonstrates his moral strands not through arrogant display of power or luxury—his large family is rather modest—but by virtue of practising the enchantments and the ethical codes of behaviour learnt at Hogwarts. Antithetical to Harry's trio, we find the gang of snobbish Draco Malfoy, Crabble and Goyle, whose racism and prejudices remind one of the class conflicts and racial discrimination. It comes as no surprise then that they are affiliated to the dark forces.

The solidarity amid pupils reveals the pedagogical texture and emphasises the function of training; in the first volume of the series, Harry is considered as a sort of destined mighty wizard, even before studying witchcraft and such burden of expectations may appear as a hindrance. Yet the meaning of robust friendship enhances the process of coming to terms with life and tackling novelty. When Harry pronounces the forbidden name of Voldemort, silence and uneasiness loom over the students but Rom tries to support his friend: Ron gasped.

'What?' said Harry.

'You said You-Know—Who's name!' said Ron, sounding both socked and impressed. 'I'd have thought you, of all people—'

'I'm not trying to be brave or anything, saying the name.' said Harry. 'I just never knew I shouldn't, see what I mean? I've got loads to learn... I bet', he added, voicing for the first time something that he'd been worrying him a lot lately, 'I bet I'm the worst in the class.'

'You wont' be. There's loads of people who come from the Muggle families and they learn quickly enough (HPPS: 75-76).

Such minor episode shows in a twin manner the significance of relationships between the two students, and children in general: on the one hand, it reduces the discourse of expectations—Ron sincerely sympathises with Harry—while on the other it stresses the educational factor as an indispensable equipment for challenging life in its mundane aspect. Oscillating from literature to pedagogy, Rowling sanctions again the connection betwixt and between education, growth and writing in a complex system of correspondences: learning, a salient aspect of the process of growing, helps Harry and his fellows to respond to the threat of Voldemort.

The idea of competition, implied in physical activities, is exploited by the Scottish novelist in her texts through the creation of Quidditch, a very popular sport amongst wizards. Combining characteristics of soccer, basketball and even cricket, it is played by two teams of seven members on flying broomsticks: three Chasers, who have to throw a ball called Quaffle into a hoop to score a goal, two Beaters, who have to cub two small balls called Bludgers, one Keeper and one Seeker, who has to catch a small flying ball called the Golden Snitch. Quidditch, behind the colourful robes of the various houses, is an outlet for the children's energies and emotions, but Rowling adds further details so that it 'lightly mocks the essentially ludicrous construction of most games while also making use of it as a showcase for Harry's magical supremacy (Eccleshare: 75). The game is actually a real psychomotor euphoria that invests the phase of childhood and communicates a shapeless vigorous whimsicality (Eccleshare: 41). Significantly, Harry is given a fundamental role: he is the Seeker because, as an adolescent, he is always involved in some kind of quest, in search for his story or identity. Catching the Golden Snitch then is a narrative image that betokens acquiring full awareness and maturity. The Quidditch championship stresses the vital worth of action, which is used not only to achieve real ends but also to define the specific person one is in terms of gestures and expressions. Whereas Harry learns how to master his tasks, what emerges from the text displays that every shade of feeling shows itself simply and straightforwardly through actions.

In children's fiction, the process of growing and learning may also be manipulated in a metaphor concerning the quality of creative writing and the duty of the artist who charts reality through discursive techniques. A curious short novel by Salman Rushdie, *Haroun and the Sea of Stories* (1990) articulates in the form of fable a reflection on narrative imagination. The son of a storyteller deprived of his boon, Haroun sets for an impervious other world to help his father and then learns from Iff, a Water Genie, about the source of all stories and anecdotes, conceived as a foaming stream, a watery wholeness that generates narratives of all types: 'Different parts of the Ocean contained different sorts of stories, and as all the stories that had ever been told and many that were still in the process of being invented could be found here, the Ocean of the Streams of Story was in fact the biggest library of the universe (72). Rushdie employs the stylistic modes of children's literature to build up a repository of stories, that points to the emergence of the author's intellectual freedom as well. What juxtaposes the postcolonial writer with Rowling resides in a literary strategy that matches tradition and modernity, and the adventures of Haroun and Harry, in spite of their delicate features, are made extemporal and extrapolated from specific contexts. Whereas Rushdie's novel is clearly derived from the classic collection of stories in Sanskrit verses written by Somadevi in the 11th century A.D. (Aklujkar: 1-12). The creator of Harry Potter is affected by Western rhetorical and narrative traditions, from Victorian times onwards to contemporary writers of children's books like Enid Blyton and Roald Dahl.

The great popularity achieved by both texts and their inter textual potentiality—*Haroun and the Sea of Stories* has been made into a BBC animated cartoon while the Harry Potter films have obtained a huge success as a globalising social and cultural phenomenon—is an evident indication that of the fermenting status of narrative for adolescents. In the specific case of Rowling then, the current issues of childhood and pedagogic approach have moulded the literary co-ordinates of Harry Potter's cycle. In such a revitalised context, young readers may dream to partake of incredible adventures while they progressively constitute their own identity and character: Rowling's fictional structures eventually become a multi-layered arena of speculations in which children's fantasy and the rationality of adults play side by side.

References

Rowling, J.K. 1997. HPPS, *Harry Potter and the Philosophical Stone*. London: Bloomsbury.

Eccleshare, Julia. 2002. *A Guide to the Harry Potter Novels*. London: Continuum.

Ricci, Rita. 2002. *Harry Potter: l'avventura di crescere. Psicologia dell' adolescenza e magia della fiaba Rome*: EDUP.

Hocke, Martin. 1989. *The Ancient Solitary Reign*. London: Grafton Books. 114-15. The other two novels are *The Lost Domain* (1993) and *Am an Owl* (1995).

Salman Rushdie. 1990. *Haroun and the Sea of Stories*. London: Puffin Books. Aklujkar, Vidyut. 1993. '*Haroun and the Sea of Stories*: Metamorphosis of an Old Metaphor' in *Commonwealth Novel in English*, Vol. 6, Number 1 & 2, Spring & Fall.

12

Bunty and the 'Loss of Garden'

Shubha Dwivedi

Just like Adam and Eve, who lost 'Eden', the garden of heavenly father, Bunty also lost or was rather dispossessed of his metaphorical 'Eden' signifying parental love and protection of a family life. In relation to Bunty, the loss of garden implies loss of childhood and loss of ceremonies of innocence.

In Mannu Bhandari's problem centric novel *Bunty*, garden is a powerful motif. Love for garden suggests not merely a somantic zest for life but a search of substitutes for lost human relationship. Bunty's 'loss of garden' is an archetypal theme through which Bhandari has projected the complex world-view of an isolated child who happens to be an individual in his own right unlike Mary's imaginary garden which has 'Silver bells and cocks and shells'. Bunty's garden is real and has real beautiful plants and trees like Raat-ki-rani and Karonda from where he offers real fruits to his Mummy in order to alleviate her unhappiness. Just like Eggerson's garden in *The Confidential Clerk,* Bunty's garden is every inch real from where he can offer beautiful things to his acquaintances. Bunty belongs to his garden and his garden belongs to him just as a child belongs to his parents. This garden helps Bunty in his solitude and it symbolises the search for harmony, peace, love and happiness in family relationships. It is a heaven where Bunty caresses each bush, each bud, each sapling and washes, cleans and protects each plant. Bunty's well-cased garden is a foil to his family which has become a 'Waste land'. Bunty deserves the same kind of love and protection from his parents which he showers on his own child like plants and trees. Bunty's garden is not an escape route to his 'private world' rather it is much in co-ordination with the world outside for others can enter this garden anytime provided they do not wish to harm his plants. Bunty is the center of that garden and feels all the responsibility towards those who are dependent on him.

Bhandari has an authentic vision of childhood and her novel enacts the development of innocence through a totally corrupt world. Bunty is a child but his sensitivity, his grief and his alienation have a disturbing effect on the adult readers and parents as the child's eye-view though bewildered, flummoxed at times, yet controvertibly makes a subtle remark on the ways of the world. Bunty has an appeal for children. It is a plea for their natural right to be treated as individuals and not to be seen as obstacles and appendages to parental ambition. Given a wider scope and outlook, Bunty can be classified as a 'social novel' for it is quite vocal about contemporary values, fallen family system and brings those wrongs to our recognition that cannot be helped by mere exposure and reform. The valuelessness in adults, and the potential heartlessness, the depravity and the cold isolation of the parents of disintegrated families are repeatedly exposed. The social claims and intentions of the novel make it a propitious tract for the modern times.

Bunty is not a record of amusing boyish adventures as one can find in the *Adventures of Tom Sawyer or Huckleberry Finn* because here the hero is a precocious child, who is deprived of all his pranks, fun and frolic early in life. Bhandari has hereby laid bare the ugly realities behind all human relationships. Bunty appears in the very nick of time and makes very subtle comments on the fast changing family scene in modern Indian society where divorce rates are on the increase day-by-day. Here, the picture of childhood is sharply in contrast with that of Ruskin Bond's where the free spirit or rather jungle-spirit is given free vent in children for their natural growth and such an atmosphere is encouraged where they get the best possible 'Wordsworthian education' in the lap of nature. In Bhandari's novel, child is an indispensable chord of the familial nexus which is every second about to wrack and ruin. In Bhandari's world-view, children are part of a 'total agony' as they bear the burden of the whole civilization and culture that is in shambles. Bhandari's Bunty is nearer to Mulk Raj Anand's Munnu because both the authors share their humanitarian concerns while dealing with the theme of lost and tormented childhood.

Mannu Bhandari cannot be considered a pessimist for bringing into light the isolation, the tortured conscience and the fear of solitude in a child's heart. She is aptly describing the 'negative values' (to use Eliot's term) of a nuclear family where a child is wanted but not reared up with responsibility. Bhandari's understanding of life and relationship is comprehensive and she is painfully aware that children like Bunty who long for happiness and parental security are untimely transformed into boys over-burdened by circumstances. Bunty is a solitary character who is not an orphan but the fact that his parents are divorced, has assigned him an orphan like situation. After the divorce of his parents, he is terrifically detached and becomes consciously aware of his own self and his surroundings. He becomes a mute observer as he is given the status of a non-entity in the lives of his parents. The boyish life of Bunty talks about two important themes: broken family relationships and the 'space' of a growing child in a disintegrated family system.

Just like Ranji, Mohinder and Koki from Ruskin Bond's *Big Business,* Bunty too has childish desires, he too can throw tantrums over trifles, but his childish temperament is subdued and curbed under the strict discipline of Shakun. Before reaching the status of an adolescent he goes through several mental, physical, familial and social traumas which hamper his natural growth. Now he cannot swing against his Mummy's arms, he cannot sleep resting his head in her lap, he is not to be consoled and pampered like a small baby and he cannot cling to his mother off and on for the fear of being called a shy girl. While he is restrained in terms of parental love because of the constant absence of his father, the fact that he is a growing up male child puts more bars on his freedom. His Vakeel chacha and his father want him to stay in a hostel and to play outdoor games and to widen his friendship sphere beyond the tiny circle of Teetu, Shanno and Kinni. Several other such rules and inhibitions are put forth which involve a great deal of tension between role confusion and identity for Bunty.

Bhandari finds self centredness, hypocrisy and pride to be the chief and driving forces in the lives of adults. Bunty's complicated upbringing is wrought by his parents' egoistic attitude and because of which they are infinitely divided from each other and also from their only son. Dickens' following assertion in *Dombey and Son* stands true to its observations till date: '...not an orphan in the wide world can be so deserted as the child who is an outcast 'from a living parent's love' (203).

Bunty is burdened with premature concern and the responsibilities of a broken marriage while psychologists firmly believe in the value of communication of distress between child and parents for the smooth development of a child's social self in the case of Bunty it remains the lose point. The way in which Bunty is 'distanced' from his parents is alarming for it brings hurdles in the way of his personality development. His fear of his parent's suffering and personal disorganization makes him weak, submissive, and insecure. His anxiousness becomes intense by the early teens. Bunty who is brought up single-handedly by his mother. He seems to be a bit timid and also possessive about her. Shakun is an over attentive, domineering mother for whom Bunty is a 'precious weapon' (44) with which she can torment Ajay. Shakun uses Bunty for her strategic interest and even Ajay seems to be too occupied in his new family to think of Bunty and thus both Shakun and Ajay never come to any compromise in the interest of Bunty's well being.

In Shakun's over-bearing presence Bunty grows up to become an extremely responsible individual concerned more about his mother's happiness. His self-esteem is augmented by means of making his mother happy and this makes him think that he is very happy with his mother for if a child like Teetu constantly lives with his father he gets only rebukes, beatings and eartwistings and that his mummy showers more affection on him than Teetu's mother and father combined. Bunty's self-esteem dependent on the pleasure or pain of mother leads to all sorts of complication in his development. As a result, Bunty is incapable of taking his decisions.

Adolescence is rightly described as 'the most dramatic life transition' and 'a period of storm and stress' by G. Standing Hall in his book on adolescence. For Bunty too, this phase of life is a period of great upheaval and he struggles within and outside to keep his psychological balance. He is all the more troubled and distressed because of being a single child who is unloved, friendless and thrown prematurely into the unsympathetic adult world. Just like other adolescents, Bunty acquires the faculty of reflection and hypothetical reasoning. He feels disturbed when he gets to know about the estranged relations of his parents through neighbours. He wants to know more and more about what transpires between his parents and therefore, he ear drops when his mother and Vakil chacha are in conversation with each other. Here, Bunty is clearly denied any space in his parent's lives and he becomes his own critic and evaluates things and events on the basis of his meager information and understanding. He becomes a problem as well as a problem solver. He tries hard even though his moral reasoning fails to solve his moral dilemmas. He is unable to understand the growing intimacy between his mother and Doctor and later their marriage dispossesses him of all his peace of mind. His rivalry or to say the struggle for the possession of his mother's love with Joat and Ami fills his life with despair and repulsion against the whole world.

Shakun's indifference towards Bunty in Doctor's house and Ajay's callousness provide no sanctum for this lonely soul. Bunty's self assertion and individualism are curbed in Doctor's house which eventually take the form of 'excessive aggression'. Bunty harbours a great deal of pent up rage and his inner suffering becomes threatening, for it comes from uncontrolled, and unbearable tension. Just like other growing children Bunty is tormented by guilt conscience and is in conflict about sexuality. Mannu Bhandari is given to much 'psychological dissection' as she deals with the sexual anxieties of Bunty. With the advent of adolescene, Bunty acts more assertively and possessively towards his mother. In the changed family atmosphere of Doctor's house, Joat's company and influence are his only support while Ami proves to be his strongest rival.

The core conflict of Bunty's life lies in the search for an identity in a world of broken beliefs, broken standards and broken relationships. We can see Bunty growing up as he longs to love and to be loved and his conflicts involve more emotional flare ups than material wants.

Alongwith R.K. Narayan's Swami, Somu and Mannu of Swami and Friends Bunty also wants to have his share of adventures. Earlier while lying in bed by his mother's side he could visit unknown mountains, forests, valleys in search of mysterious Sadhus but now he has lost his childhood as well as that fairy tale world. He has lost the dream world of Sonal Rani, and also the rebukes of Phaphi, his flower beds, his affectionate mother and his doting father with the passage of time.

Bunty focuses on the sufferings of unwanted and uncared for children. The novel is about an innocent child's first acquaintances with the world. Bunty is definitely ours as the little of the Hindi novel situates it among the readers for acknowledgement by calling it *Aapka Bunty*. Bunty belongs to us, he is a part of our experiences, and moreover the problems in his life are created as well as intensified by us. Bunty is a character who wants to embrace us with both his arms and who wants to cling to those who try to get rid of him. Bunty is a child archetype who reflects the complex development of a neglected child. The novel stresses on the overriding need for the adults to understand the distress of children. Bhandari's fiction calls for the establishment of a more humane, loving and just society which will give a beautiful, well-trimmed and cared for garden to each child to bloom and blossom.

References

Bhandari, Mannu. 1983. *Bunty*, Trans. Jai Ratan. New Delhi: National Publishing House.

Dickens, Charles. 1985. Dealings with the Firm of Domby and Son, Wholesale, Retail and for Exportation, Monthly Numbers in Master Humphrey's Clock, Oct. 1846, April 1848, Penguin.

Hall, G. Stanley. 1904. New York: *Adolescene*.

Szapz S. Thomas. 1959. *The Communication of Distress between Child and Parent*. The Memorial Lecture of the Society of Medical Psychoanalysis in New York on May 13.

Eliot, T.S. 1920. *The Sacred Wood*. London: Methuen and Co. Ltd.

13

Vision of Childhood in the Poetry of Robert Frost

Awadhesh K. Mishra

Robert Frost happens to be a twentieth century poet of immense popularity. His first volume of poems was published in 1915 and the last one in 1964. He lived through a troubled and tension-ridden age, which is usually known as 'the modern age'. Frost has been called the purest classical poet of today'. He is placed beside Emerson, Howthorn and Thoreau. But Frost's poetry does not show the all-embracing philosophic grasp of Emerson, Thoreau and Whitman. He does not imbibe different cultures and creeds like those writers. He does not show a concern for death or an obsession with religious faith which Emily Dickinson does with her visionary insight into the mystery of human existence. In point of time, he is contemporary of Eliot, Yeats and Auden. He has not pointed to the coffee-house of visiting lover and beloved with learned allusions, ironic contrasts and complex symbols of T.S. Eliot. Still, his poetry is modern in its spirit and tone. As pointed out by Frosher, Modernity is related to certain attitudes of experience and expression in which the problems are dealt with the might of childhood.

Frost's love of experimentation in his early period of creative life is full of exercise of being poet. The childhood period is given prominence and the poet displays the mysterious sense of wonder that comes to a child lying awake. In the poem 'In a vale', the poet fashions a story out of old longings. A single stanza from the poem would be sufficient to witness these facts:

When I was young, we dwelt in a vale
Bay a misty pen that range all night,
And thus it was the maidens pale
I knew so well, whose garments trail
Across the reach to a window light.

The ability to reflect atmosphere, to merge the inner feeling with the outer, is quite prominent is his lyric 'Love and Question'. It is an effective example of young feature even if it is present in the very first volume of his poetry.

The approach of the childhood in modern age is all fresh as he looks towards a state of international relationship where no barrier would be present. His suggestions are quite lively:

Before I built a wall I'd ask to know what I was walling in or walling out,
And to whom I was like to give offense.

In Frost's poems we find deeper thoughts about the childhood feeling that talks about the nature. Nature is like a loyal friend that remains forever with us to offer us company. 'A Girl's Garden' may be discussed for its deeper thought on childhood. The girl offers her father to become a farmer herself. In reply the father says:

That ought to make you
An ideal one girl farm
And give you a chance to put some strength
on your slim jim arm.

Thus the girl started and worked by her own hands for fame. One could find a variety of vegetables in her farm:

Her crops miscellany
When all was said and done,
A little bit of everything,
A great deal of none.

Here she makes it 'A little bit of everything,' and when she compares her farm with all other farms in the village she finds a great deal of difference:

Now when she sees in the village
How village things go,
Just when it seem to come in right
She says, I know!

The attitude displays the task of the girl and to some extent the belief of the poet. When the girl tells her tale twice to anybody she does not commit a crime. She does not feel shy. She knows it better that such type of story would plant here childhood into adultness and start a new phase in her life. That scope is always available to human beings in this world.

In another poem 'Out Out' the poet describes the tragedy of childhood. Here's the tragic story of a boy that ends the poem in affirmation, telling how the process of life must go on. The poem begins with a boy who moves here and there for work. Before the scheduled time he cannot call it a day as he has many things to do. A boy really feels happy if he can finish his work before time. This boy does not have the opportunity. The setting sun provides a kind of setting for the tragedy of the boy. His life would have finished his work soon. However, the body could not escape the inevitable, his hand was already gone. His cry is heart-touching when he tells his sister;

Don't let him cut my hand off/the doctor, when he comes Don't let him sister.' The tragic atmosphere becomes tense when the poet describes the 'big boy/doing a man's work, though a child at heart.' At last the body died, but cleverly the speaker of the poem turns to describe the prevailing atmosphere. One may die, but others keep on going:

'—And they, since
Where not the one dead, turned to their affairs.'

Death is a part of child's life, yet the child must look forward and cross the darker aspect of life. Frost is an expert in understanding of life. The poet makes virtually no comments and because of this he is able to create a sharper sense of the suddenness of the tragedy and its stark horror. In Shakespeare's *Macbeth*, Macbeth, hearing of his wife's death, soliloquizes.

Out, out brief candle!
Life's but a walking shadow, a poor player
That shuts and frets his/hour upon the stage
And then is heard no more, It is a tale
Told by an idiot, full of sound and fury,
Signifying nothing.

Macbeth here speaks of the meaninglessness of life, its senselessness and its purposelessness. Frost's poem, 'The Violent Death of the Youth' raises similar questions as to a life's value. The sowing has proceeded routine, nothing makes the day unique, Nothing happened: the day was all but done.' At this point, the poet breaks:

Call it a day, I wish they might have said
To please the boy giving him the half hour
That a boy counts so much when saved from work.

Through these words, the speaker emphasizes the youthful quality of the child and by so doing he prepares the reader for a sense of the tragedy of one dying so young. There is a suggestion of the idea that a child ought not to be forced to work so long. When the entire poem is read, one feels that if the other workers might have recognized his desire for play and let him stop early, the tragedy might not have occurred. When his sister tells the lawyers that supper is ready, the child anxiously and carelessly drops the power-saw which, in falling, cut into his wrist. Frost says in horror of the incident.

As if to prove saws knew what supper meant.
Leapet out at the boys hand, or seemed to leap
He must have given the hand.
However it was.
Neither refused the meeting. But the hand!'

Only a boy, he is mature enough to see that the loss of his hand represents the loss of a part of himself. His life is flawed. He will never be able to saw again, and do child's work again. He will not be able to fulfill himself. It is for this reason he dies, not because of the physical shock of his wound.

They listened at his heart.
Little-less-nothing: and they ended it.

Besides these poems the metaphorical poems like 'The Telephone' and 'Birches' enlarge the scope of his image. The game of a boy provides the poet with a meaning that he would like to achieve in his own life. So the final section of the poem shows the identification of the poet with the boy. 'So as I once myself a swinger of birches/ And so I dream of going back to be'.

In the lines that follow, Frost gives a realistic description of the ice on birch trees: how the branches are weighted down, how the ice cracks and shatters like glass on the crusty snow, and how the trees are permanently bent but unbroken. Years after years of ice storm they bent their branches down to the ground like a kneeling girl's hair cascades to the ground before her. He imagines that the trees have been bent by a boy who is too far from town to play baseball and who therefore has learnt to play by himself. He sees his father's birches as objects to be conquered, and he views climbing them as an art. It shows the psychology of children particularly of boys to behave like adults.

He learnt all there was
To learn about not launching out too soon
And so not carrying the tree away clear to the ground.

Climbing is performed skillfully and precisely. He performs each action as carefully as though it were as delicate an operation as filling a cup to the brim.

It becomes apparent that Frost regards his explanation of the shape of the trees as the best one because it represents artistic, challenging, and self-reliant aspect of a young boy. It shows how he is rooted in the soil and is not mere alien. 'I'd like to get away from earth awhile 'but' earth is the right place for love: I don't know where it's likely to go better'.

Baseball comes to be emblematic of all that adds to and sharpens the spirit of completion while swinging on birches reveals a spontaneity that is only given to the boy who went out to fetch the cows. Thus the poem is complete identification between the labour and, the boy and his instrument, the soul and the body. The poem also reveals that Frost demands an amplitude spread, and depth in life, in habits, in dwelling and also in physique.

'The Subverted Flower' is a natural grouping poem, which gives somewhat different vision of the poet and that of the girl. We see that the girl has resisted the advance of the boy which she has apparently invited by presenting him with a flower. The boy is struggling under the stress of strong emotion but is nevertheless tender and solicitous. 'He smiled for her to smile' his arms 'ache' to touch her neck and hair 'to Clasp' but 'not to harm'. The girl however is 'either blind or willfully unkind' and in either case is unmoved until she hears him speak his tentative yearning words.

The boy's words make the transition to the girl's point of view. She 'thought' she heard him say words, but all she can see is the stress of passion which makes him appear to her an animal. She thinks she hears him say certain words. She feels that she had to learn away, she dared not stir, 'because it might arouse him.' The mothers call makes her steal a look and the boy appears like an animal to her. The flower and by implication the boys feelings, are 'base and fated' because she has made them so.

Frost believes that poetry should have a wildness, by which he means a freshness and vitality, a sense of exhilaration and discovery. A work intriguingly leads the readers to a thematic conclusion. The challenge that the poet faces is to achieve as much variety as possible within limitation. In order for the sense of discovery to be achieved, Frost believes that the poet must have freedom to choose his material. He cannot be forced to look for connections in life. Rather, he must be somewhat passive, allowing experience to come to him, never requiring it to yield hidden meanings, but always allowing it to make its own connections in due time. He contrasts the poet's process with that of a scholar.

'Scholars and artists thrown together are often annoyed at the puzzle of where they differ. Both work from knowledge, but I suspect they differ most importantly in the way their knowledge is come by. Scholars get theirs with conscientious thoroughness along projected lines of logic: They stick to nothing deliberately but let what will stick to them like burrs where they walk in the fields. No acquirement is on assignment, or even self-assignment.

By exercising a wise passiveness the poet's will, in due time, comes to discover childhood piece of knowledge picked up like burrs. The poet and reader both must share the excitement and surprise of discovering a truth, which, is most important.

No surprise for the writer, no surprise for the reader, for me the initial delight is the surprise of remembering something I did not know I knew.... It must be a revelation or series of revelation as much for the poet as for the reader.'

14

Children and Associated Problems

Neha Nigam

Childhood development presents a pattern similar to that of the history of mankind. As the child grows he faces restraints and prohibiti ›ns imposed by his parents. Unless parental behaviour is exceptionally improper, the child will become more and more independent as he grows.

Gradually the ties connecting him with his parents become weaker as he develops more awareness of his individuality. This process of development brings about dangers similar to those in the history of mankind, for a higher level of individualization is accompanied by a decline in security feeling. The little child does not have much freedom, but he is happy and secure in his dependence on his parents. Maturity means more independence, but it also means less security than in childhood. Children who have been reared by hostile on domineering parents will be less prepared to face the problem of maturity and they may feel powerless, forsaken and isolated. Not only defense mechanism but the totality of the child's character is melded by his parents. Families usually serve as psychological agents of the society and transmit the cultural values of their nation and class to the children. The child's character is formed by social and cultural patterns as represented by the characters of his parents. The child's individual character is a product of the specific environmental influences exercised by his parents.

Child rearing practices that influence character foundation are not only the feelings of the child and teaching him to control his bowels but the total sum of social relationships at home. If the home situation encourages friendliness and acceptance, the child is likely to develop the receptive dependent personality traits. Her/His childhood experiences will teach her/ him that s/he got the most out of complying with others in trying to please them. If the child receives everything only after a quarrel, a fight or a period of stubbiness, s/he will probably develop the oral-aggressiveness or exploiting sadistic character. The child who grows up in a home atmosphere of 'grab it' will probably follow this pattern of behaviour all his life. In a home where scarcity, distrust and suspicion prevail, the child will learn to keep what s/he gets and not let people take away anything that belongs to her/him.

Six Epochs in Personality Developments

Developmental stages of personality are distinguished into six epochs by a psychologist Sullivan.

The first developmental stage is infancy, which starts at birth and continues until the maturation of the capacity for language. The newborn child strives for unrestricted satisfaction of his needs and unlimited expression of her/his power. Both tendencies meet with a certain type of response from the mother. She may approve or disapprove of the behaviour of the child. Since it is up to her to satisfy her/him or to deny satisfaction, the infant lessons to adjust her/himself to her/his mother at an early stage. This process of adjustment takes place because of the child's ability to feel somehow her/his mother's state of mind. Empathy is the non-verbal way of communicating emotion. The mother's approval is conducive to a euphoric state in the child while the mother's disapproval may produce anxiety.

Sooner or later the infant learns to relate her/his pleasant feeling of euphoria or the annoying feeling of anxiety to her/ his own behaviour. Some of her/his activities are somehow connected with euphoria while others cause anxiety. S/he learns to perceive the signs of approval or disapproval to act accordingly.

The infant develops three types of personifications of her/himself. When her/his behaviour is accepted and praised, s/he develops self-identification or approval. In infancy the child begins to develop personification of other people too. The feeling of euphoria is conducive to a 'good mother' personification, while anxiety states bring 'bad mother' personifications.

The second developmental stage is childhood. Childhood is an era of most pervasive adulation processes. The child learns toilet habits, eating habits, cleanliness and most of the habitual ways of behaviour regarded as proper by the society and represented by her/his parents. The child learns how to restrain her/his drive for power. Many of her/his activities are frustrated or prohibited by parents. Some of the unacceptable desires are sublimated. The child's efforts to get approval meet with parental lack of patience, fatigue or some other kind of rejecting behaviour. This may lead to distortions of the reality of child, the child who craves parental love and receives nothing but rejection may develop paranoid distortions. S/he may regard her/himself as lonely and rejected in a cold and hostile world. The child may then try to alleviate her/his anxiety by producing anger.

The juvenile era starts in civilization with school age. The child manifests a shift from contentment in an environment of totalitarian adults toward an environment of persons significantly like her/him. Meeting other children encourages interpersonal validation of perception and leads gradually to the syntactic mode. The child learns to pay more attention to the opinions of other children, s/he tries to become popular and fears to be alone or even worse, rejected by her/his group. The child's process of socialization leads towards the establishment of personal friendship with one or more children. Pre-adolescence starts between the age of 8 to 12. It is characterized by the appearance of the capacity to love. In this era most people develop consensual validation by exchange of words and ideas with their friends. Adolescence is an era of patterning of lustful behaviour.

Language Development

The common assumption is that the child learns to speak by imitation. By mimicking what her/his parents say and practicising these speech forms, s/he gradually modifies her/his speech until it appropriates adult language. Under the impetus of recent work in linguistic and psycholinguistics, a different picture of child language has emerged. This new view proposes certain innate, or built-in mechanisms for processing language which enable the child to construct her/his own rules for language usage. These rules form the child's theory of new language works, the child modifies her/his theory until s/he arrives at one that permits her/him to connect and generate adult language. Thus all normal children acquire a native language, it is that not a child must be taught.

Stages of Language Development

(i) **Babbling and initial words.** During the first month of life, vocalization is very limited but at about six months infants begin to produce an immense variety of sounds in increasingly complex combinations. This repetition of the syllables resembling those words used in adult speech is called babbling. Child starts experimenting with sounds. At about nine months the range of babbled sound narrows and the infants begin to concentrate on those sounds that will appear in her/his first word.

(ii) **Grammar and meanings.** A very large number of meaningful sentences could be produced and with a few rules. Complex sentences with several clauses could be generated. It needs only a few more rules to specify the infinite number of grammatical sentences possible in a language. A very important part of the language development consists of learning the rules of grammar that children use so effortlessly and without conscious awareness is constructing sentences to impress what they want to say.

(iii) **Words and meaning.** If the child produces a sound that approximates a word—the parents may hasten to provide the food, thus increasing the likelihood that the child will produce a similar sound when hungry. By three or four years of age the child's over extensions of meaning are less obvious, but closely related words may still be confused. Children acquire the meaning of words by a gradual process of discrimination, proceeding from those more general features that characterize the word to specific ones.

(iv) Primitive sentences. After the child has acquired the modest vocabulary, s/he begins to form sentences. Eventually s/he must comprehend long, complicated sentences and produce such sentences on his own. Speech at this stage of development (two years) has been termed telegraphic. The child usually preserves the order of the parent's speech but leaves out the less important words or word parts. At this stage of language development the child comprehends much more than s/he can express.

(v) Complex sentences. Children progress rapidly from two words utterances to more complex sentences. Children seem to be developing their own rules system in a gradual approach to the adult system. Children acquire general rules in learning a language and only through time and experience learn to modify these rules to accommodate exceptions.

The Parent Figure (Primary Group)

The earliest group that everyone experiences is the family and the first leader with whom we become acquainted are our parents. Go on to school, teacher takes on parental rule. There is a tendency, particularly during childhood and adolescence, in us to regard all authority figure in somewhat the same way as we regard our parents. There are two main types of parental leaders. One is the dominating, forbidding, punishing, demanding, the authoritarian, leader called father figure. The other is the housing, sheltering, understanding, supportive, reassuring, leader called mother figure.

Primary groups are those in which interpersonal relationships take place on a face-to-face basis and with great frequency. The major characteristics of primary groups, according to Cooley, are the influence they have in forming the social nature and ideals of the individual. Families are the most obvious example of primary groups.

PROBLEMS

FACTORS RESPONSIBLE FOR ABNORMAL BEHAVIOUR IN CHILDREN

Abnormal Behaviour

Abnormal behaviour means psychological handicap. It is the abnormalities of psycho motor function, perception, cognition, motivation, emotion as well as abnormalities of serial-behaviour and personalities.

Causes of Abnormal Behaviour

(1) **Malnutrition.** Severe malnutrition during infancy not only impairs physical development but also lowers body resistance, affects brain growth and the growth of intelligence in children.

(2) **Inadequate mothering.** Inadequate mothering as manifested in the terms of indifferent and rejecting attitude or a punishing nature, may cause tense, unsatisfied and negative behaviour among infants.

(3) **The inadequate family.** A family which is facing problems due to lack of financial, physical and psychological resources, cannot provide their children with the safety and security they need and the competencies they require.

(4) **The antisocial family.** In some families, parents overtly engage in behaviour that is antisocial. They may set negative models for their children.

(5) **Broken home.** Loss of the father is more traumatic for a son than for a daughter. Feelings of insecurity and rejection may be aggravated by conflicting loyalties. Sometimes by scolding the child silences her/him. While staying with one or other parent in case of divorce or separation also affects negatively.

(6) **Neglected by parents.** When the children are neglected by their parents they develop a pessimistic attitude and lose all charm in life. S/he may develop the habit of crying for nothing. The social and mental development of such a child is obstructed.

(7) **High expectations of parents.** Some parents place very high ideals before their children and they fail to understand whether the children have the physical, social, mental and emotional merits for the same or not. Parents are usually disappointed at the performance of their children. The children also feels depressed and develop inferiority complex.

(8) **Lack of a uniform discipline at a home.** Some parents are not able to maintain a uniform discipline in relations with their children. Sometimes they punish their children for a certain thing and at another time they happen to praise them for the same. Some parents present wrong examples before their children. Children usually consider their parents as their models. At such behaviour of parents children get confused and they fail to understand the ideal that they should follow.

(9) **Inadequate mutual response.** Children must be able to talk freely with their parents on matters that concern them and regarding their personality development. When the children are not able to express their feeling to their parents they experience an inner conflict which is harmful to a smooth emotional development.

(10) **Genetic Factors.** The genetic syndromes affect adversely the intellectual or physical capabilities and also the physical appearance of the victim. The genetic defects arise partly due to the function of the dominant on recessive genes leading to mental retardation. Thus important genetic syndromes are Down's syndrome and Phenyl Ketonuria.

(a) ***Down's Syndrome.*** It is also known as mongolism, and is caused by chromosomal aberrations. It was Langdon Down who first described this syndrome in 1886. About ten per cent of the moderately and severely retarded children suffer from Down's syndrome. The physical abnormalities of children are flat face, irregular teeth, small skull etc. The general majority of mongoloid children have 47 chromosomes instead of usual 46. The older the mother, the greater is the risk of her/him bearing a mongoloid.

(b) ***Phenyl Ketoneuria.*** It was first described by Folling in 1935. It is caused due to genetic error. Here the enzymes responsible for the metabolism of the biochemical phenyl alanine is not present at birth. As a result, severe brain damages are produced.

(11) Maternal infection. According to Hellman and Pritdrard (1971), five per cent of the pregnancies may be accompanied by some viral infection having their dangerous effects upon the unborn during the first 3 months. Due to this infection, certain damaging agents get in causing measles, chickenpox, small pox etc.

(12) Premature birth. Babies under 5.5 pound birth weight suffer from several physical and mental difficulties.

(13) Anoxia. Lack of oxygen during the birth process may lead to mild retardation.

(14) Kernicterus. Due to dysfunction of the liver in the new born this disease occurs which leads to mental retardation.

Treatment of Mentally Retarded Child

It is basically not a medical problem. It can be checked if the social attitude can be changed and the required social condition can be stimulated.

(1) Educating parents. Because of personality difficulties and the problems of adjustment of the retarded child, many parents consider their life to be miserable, and thus ignore the retarded child. The parents therefore should be properly trained as to how to handle the mentally retarded child.

(2) Special education for the retarded. Special education provides reasonable help to educate mentally retarded children.

(3) Residential placement. Residential placement deals with the total control of the retarded person's life, her/his private and personal experiences. It removes the retarded persons from their home environment and places them in an artificially made environment suitable for their personality development.

(4) Health of expectant mother. Expectant mothers should be given all the necessary care in order to prevent any untoward happening.

(5) **Services of obstetrician.** Obstetricians will be of great help for preventing any undesirable feature at the time of pregnancy.

(6) **Research Program.** Through certain research, deviations in the combination of chromosomes should be identified.

Juvenile Delinquency (children crime). Children and adolescents who commit crime under statutory age are referred to as delinquents. The maximum age limit varies, but in most states offenders under 16 or 18 are classified as Juvenile delinquents.

Court Act. A delinquent child is one who has violated any law of the commonwealth or ordinance of the city; a child who by reason of being wayward or habitually disobedient, is uncontrolled by his parents, guardian, custodian or legal representative, a child who is habitually truant at school or home, a child who habitually so departs himself as to injure or endanger the morals or health of her/himself or others. In large metropolitan areas about two per cent of the children of school age are referred each year to juvenile courts as alleged delinquents and one per cent of the school age population are adjudged delinquents.

FACTORS IN CRIME

(I) Biological Factors

(a) **Heredity.** More than fifty per cent of the adult offenders studied by the Gulecks came from families having a criminal record.

(b) **Physical Findings.** During the last part of 19th century, Lombnoso, an Italian physician, advanced the theory that criminals possessed a greater number of physical traits of an atavistic or apelike nature than general population.

(II) Social Disorganization

In both primitive and contemporary society, the stability of social order is an important controlling factor in incidence of crime. Social disorganization, dislocation of population and slum areas do not cause crime but they indirectly encourage criminality by increasing opportunities for antisocial behaviour. The family life of delinquents is characterized by disorganization, discord and general instability.

(III) Economic Aspects

The majority of delinquents come from poor homes and are either unemployed or engaged in unskilled and low-income occupations. The low economic status of the criminal may be an incentive to offences against property and prosperity.

(IV) Race

Cultural traditions and restrictions, together with environmental influences may increase or decrease the frequency of law violations and determine the nature of offences committed by a particular racial group.

(V) Psychological and Psychiatric Factors

(a) Intelligence: The intelligence of apprehended criminals and delinquents is lower than general population. Most delinquents are poorly educated and come from poor cultural areas.

(b) Neuroses: Personality inventories and clinical observations indicate that delinquents are more neurotic than general population.

(c) Psychopathic personality: Psychopathic personality includes pathological liars, sexual perverts, tramps, amoral individuals and certain types of emotionally unstable individuals. The types of crimes committed by these individuals do not differ greatly from those of prisoners.

Treatment of Criminals

(1) Many first offenders are accidental criminals who break the law by chance. If sent to prisons, these individuals are frequently converted to a life of crime as a result of their association with hardened criminals and by exposure to the unfavourable influence of the prisons regime. If they are kept out of prison and carefully supervised by competent probation officer, they usually become law-abiding citizens.

(2) Prisoners vary in the type of supervision and training

they require. Psychotic and mentally defective prisoners are best confined for long periods in Special institutions. Some convicts, including incorrigibles, require maximum custody, other respond best of given minimum custody.

(3) More humane treatment needs to be given in prison. Harsh treatment in prison often destroys all that is good in wo/man and leads to embitterment towards society. The modern policy is to treat prisoners like human beings.

(4) General improvement in custodial care, social service work, medical and psychiatric treatment, classification, religious guidance and other professional services greatly help. This has been largely brought about by the introduction of competitive civil services examination and the adoption of merit system for appointments and promotions.

Treatment of Juvenile Delinquents. When referred to court, children are usually examined informally. The emphasis is upon understanding and helping the individual child rather than punishing him. Many cases are disposed of unofficially through interviews and conferences with the parties concerned. The more serious cases are tried in juvenile courts. Depending on the nature of the offense and the past history of the offender, the judge may dismiss the delinquent with a warning, place him on probation, or sentence him to a reformatory, industrial school or camp. Close to fifty per cent of cases disposed of by juvenile courts each year are dismissed or adjusted. Between thirty to thirty five per cent are placed on probation or otherwise supervised, ten per cent are committed to correctional institutions for indefinite periods, and the remaining cases are settled in other ways.

In most aware and modern institutions today, delinquents have considerable freedom, are well cared for physically, receive adequate educational and vocational training, and are given an opportunity to engage in recreational and social activities. As soon as feasible, they are released to the custody of parole officers and civic groups, who assume responsibility for continuing the rehabilitation program in the community.

Prevention of Crime

(1) **The Development of Wholesome Personalities in Childhood.** The roots of crime are deeply embeded in the early history of the individual. Parents may discourage antisocial tendencies in their children by maintaining a favourable emotional atmosphere in the home, establishing friendly relations with their children and carefully guiding their moral and character development. In the later task, the religious agencies, the school and the scout movement may also play important roles.

(2) **The Early Discovery and Treatment of Potential Delinquents and Criminals.** Individuals do not become criminals overnight. Their history is one of gradual movement. Development of criminal careers could be cut short by prompt detection and guidance in the early stages.

(3) **The elimination of factors that favour crime.** Within the category may be placed the removal of children from undesirable homes, the elimination of slum areas, the expansion of recreational facilities to provide wholesome activity outlets for under-privileged children and the organization of girls/boys clubs to counteract the influence of gangs.

(4) **Vigilant supervision and strict law enactment.** The temptation to commit a crime is normally counterbalanced by fear of arrest and conviction. A potential offender will take a chance if s/he runs little risk of being apprehended and imprisoned but s/he will frequently inhibit her/his criminal impulses if she realises that she cannot get away with it. A strong, efficient police force and a strict court system will deter many borderline cases from criminal behaviour.

(5) **Good government and legal reforms.** To many communities, the incidence of certain types of crime may be radically reduced by breaking the corrupt alliance that exists between crime and politics. The prohibition experiment provides a good example of how laws may influence crime. At present, many white collar criminals manage to evade punishment because of inadequate laws.

15

A Comparison of the Childhood of Mahatma Gandhi and Adolf Hitler

Kiran Shukla

"The great thing in the world in not so much where we stand as in what direction we are moving." Time, the best maker of a mind, leads a person to develop according to own social circumstances. It presents instances of great happenings, creates great and inspiring persons and thus makes a history. A child comes to the existence facing different circumstances, grows and possibly becomes some great figure, if benefited by the time. Childhood is the time that leads a person to have a steady nature. The social circumstances, family background, social and historical happenings, peculiar traditions etc., all these affect human brain to lead a life having a firm nature. It is quite possible that the impression of the total set up of the society make a child a great person. And there become one Adolf Hitler and one Mahatma Gandhi. Both are the best instances having different aspects of nature. These two personalities changed the course of history by their diagonally different natures, played a main role in leading their nations. They were the need of their time and nations. Both are successful though actions were just opposite to each other, the one following non-violence and the other violence. The most thought-provoking question is that how the two personalities were so much different as of the two banks of a river which never meet. What is the reason behind general impression that when we speak of Gandhi, we think of 'Ahimsa' and when we speak of Hitler, we think of cruelty. It must be the social and historical circumstances of their childhood which changed their mind and made them different personalities. It is very interesting and thought-provoking to consider the psyche of the great leaders from their childhood by their autobiographies. These two autobiographies prove the fact that variety is the spice of life and create great interest and curiosity in reader's mind.

Gandhi's autobiography is the expression of self-introspection. He has searched himself through and through and examined and analyzed every psychological situation, whereas Hitler's autobiography is the description of his own development. It is written in order to produce more equality and uniformity in the defense of his doctrines.

Gandhi was influenced by his father and mother, even he followed those values taught to him. During his childhood Gandhi himself had been a mediocre student. As he mentions in his autobiography, 'there is hardly anything to note about my studies.' He used to be very shy and avoided all company. His books and lessons were his sole companions, rather he was introvert. As is obvious from his daily habit, when he used to be in school he remained there for the time and at the stroke of the hour he ran back home as the school closed. In this regard he himself states "I literally ran back, because I could not bear to talk to anybody. I was even afraid lest anyone should poke fun at me." He did not tell a lie even during his childhood either to his teachers or to his schoolmates. There was no question of making fun of others. His shyness, avoidance of all company, all these introversive qualities indicate that he never could be dictator like Hitler.

Hitler had been aware of the struggle of his father for his livelihood and for the better settlement. His father wished Hitler to become government official as he wished his son not to have such struggle in his life. But Hitler had a feeling of suppression by the wishes of his father. Even his way of thinking was just opposite to his father from his childhood. He did not want to spend his life in such a monotonous service. And he was not less obstinate in his decision. The two, the father and the son both were as in opposition. Hitler was aware of the fact why his father was anxious about his son to become an official of the Government. He even writes in his autobiography: "Indeed he had decided on that career for me. The difficulties through which he had to struggle in making his own career led him to overestimate what he had achieved, because this was exclusively the result of his own indefatigable industry and energy. The characteristic pride of the self-made man urged him towards the idea that his son should follow the same calling and if possible rise to a higher position in it. Moreover, this idea was strengthened by the consideration that the results of his own life's industry had placed him in a position to facilitate his son's advancement in the same career".

But Hitler was firm in his decision 'I would not become a civil servant.' How fully developed was his mind about his career and nation, his goal was clear even when he was eleven year old. No amount of persuasion and no amount of 'grave' warnings could break down that opposition, 'I would not become a State Official, not on any account.' Even when there was conflict with his father he was not agitated. Hitler was so firm and keen in his decision that even he says, "My own resolution not to become a Government official was sufficient for the time being to put my mind completely at rest." This very quality to consider the situation very keenly and stick to a firm decision from early childhood is very obvious in his personality that made him a great dictator. He thought to satisfy his father as a counter suggestion of being a painter or an artist. When he was twelve his father asked for the first time what he wanted to become and the reply was automatically expressed. As Hitler possessed the quality of obstinacy from his father along with other qualities, so his reply was equally energetic, 'But it stated something quite the contrary.' "At that our struggle became stalemate. The father would not abandon his 'Never' and I became all the more consolidated in my 'Nevertheless'.

Though he loved his father but that love could not intervene the two obstinate persons to submit. And the resulting situation was not pleasant. If his father forbade him to entertain any hopes of taking up the art of painting as a profession, Hitler went a step further and declared that he would not study anything else. His father's decision was irrevocable and the situation became more strained. His father decided to 'assert his parental authority at all costs.'

How sharp and serene minded the boy was and he knew how to tackle the situation; this is very notable point in his character, as he mentions in his autobiography, 'That led me to adopt an attitude of circumspect silence, but I put my threat into execution. I thought that, once it became clear to my father that I was making no progress at the Realschule, for weal or for woe, he would be forced to allow me to follow the happy career I had dreamed of.'

All the things went on according to his ideas. He studied just the subjects that appealed to him or might be of advantage to him later on as a painter. As far as other subjects are concerned, he completely sabotaged. The very interesting thing about his study and school reports is that they were always in the extremes of good or bad according to the subject and interest it had for him. "In one column my qualification read 'very good' or 'excellent'. In another it read 'average' or even 'below average'. But far my best subjects were geography and, even more so, general history. These were my two favourite subjects, and I led the class in them."

Hitler considered the goal of his study to become a nationalist and to learn and understand and grasp the true meaning of history. The most appealing thing in Hitler was his belief in nationalism. Through his study he was sure that he became a nationalist and he learned to understand and grasp the true meaning of history. Those days the old Austria was a multinational state. Hitler know that the citizens of the German Empire could not understand what the fact 'Multinationalism' meant in the every day life of the individuals within such a state. He had the idea that the Germans of the Reich did not realize that the Germans in Austria had been the best racial stock. Only very few of the Germans in the Reich itself had an idea of the bitter struggle which those Eastern Germans had to carry on daily for the preservation of their German language, their German schools and their German character.

There was a language fight which was carried on in the old Austria. The fight was waged in its bitterest form around the school. The reason of this fight in the school, Hitler depicts very beautifully. As his mind was engrossed with natural thoughts "...because this was the nursery where the seeds had to be watered which were to spring up and form the future generation. The tactical objective of the fight was the winning over of the child, and it was to the child that the first rallying cry was addressed." "German youth, do not forget that you are a German", and "Remember, little girl, that one day you must be a German mother."

'Those who know something of the juvenile spirit can understand how youth will always lend a glad ear to such a rallying cry.' The very keen observer Hitler also understood the result of that rallying cry. And the result was that the juvenile passion for nationalism was seen everywhere. Under many forms the young people led the struggle fighting in their own way with their weapons. The passion was so strong that they even refused to sing non-German songs. Even if they were checked away from their German allegiance, 'the more they exalted the glory of their German heroes.' They stinted themselves in purchasing things to eat to spare their pennies to help the war chest of their elders. 'They were incredibly alert to the significance of what the non-German teacher said and they contradicted in unison. They wore the forbidden emblems of their own kinsfolk and were happy when penalized for doing so or even physically punished. In miniature they were mirrors of loyalty from which the older people might learn a lesson.'

This was the passion for the nationalism and that Hitler also was keen to. He took part in the struggle which the nationalites were waging against one another in the old Austria. As the citizens of the German Austria were not aware of the nationality, the youth were taught about it politically which also inspired Hitler to become an ardent 'German National'.

Thus in the very young age of fifteen, Hitler's mind developed rapidly towards the nationalist direction. Even he understood the distinction between dynastic patriotism and nationalism based on the concept of folk or people. Though he was inclined towards the subsequent.

During the time of Hitler universal history was the subject almost exclusively taught in the Austrian school. There was no division of Germany history and Austrian history. It was closely bound up with the existence and development of Germany as a whole. But indeed when German people came to be divided between two states, this division of German history began to take place.

Hitler considered the true meaning, true application of study. As he was interested in history and was a well orator, his mind also inclined in seeking the true purpose of the study of history. "To study history means to search for and discover the forces that are the causes of those results which appear before our eyes as historical events. The art of reading and studying consists in remembering the essentials and forgetting what is not essential." This is the true essence that Hitler considered. This keen perception came as he observed the elucidation of basic facts in teaching history by his ideal teacher, Dr. Leopold Poetsch. His taking right decision at right time, doing any work with full enthusiasm alongwith eloquent power inspired Hitler to become enthusiastic in learning history and considering the facts behind the transmutation of the environment. The professor was able to capture the examples of everyday problems that agitated their minds. And the national fervour was also utilized by him while teaching. He often appealed to Hitler's sense of national honour. His inclination in pondering over the changing facts of the history and practical application of the study of history indicates a keen observant and curious mind of Hitler from very young age. Hitler in his very early years of youth came to certain conclusions and rather became more profoundly convinced of them as the years passed. They were: "That the dissolution of the Austrian Empire is a preliminary condition for the defence of Germany; further, that national feeling is by no means identical with dynastic patriotism; finally, and above all, that the House of Habsbury was destined to bring misfortune to the German nation."

Further, he asserts "As a logical consequence of these convictions, there arose in me a feeling of intense love for my German Austrian home and a profound hatred for the Austrian State."

Now Hitler's mind became set-up of the historical thinking of that kind. He considered the contemporary historical events equivalent to politics. In this respect world history became an inexhaustible source and there was less to learn in politics. Besides the World history and politics he was interested in art. The play, *William Tell* and opera *Lohengrin* inspired him when he was twelve years old. The intense interest in these subjects and the fervour of nationalism arose in him profound aversion for the career that his father had chose for him. His view became broad regarding career. He became drastically against of a job, which limited his ambitions. This impact is obvious in him from his childhood.

But the unfortunate demise of his father due to sickness, while Hitler was only of thirteen shocked him. Now he had to face the bitter reality of life which his father had faced in his life to struggle for the livelihood of the family.

His father had the strenuous struggle in his life against poverty but never gave it. He learnt to cope with the stresses and strains of public life. But then Hitler's mother felt her duty to continue his education and fulfil his father's desire. But Hitler's firm determination not to become an official of the state became profound, as he was disagree with the curriculum and teaching methods followed in the middle school. The boy Hitler's ideal education was different and rather in superficial form of its application in reforming the views of public and to raise the fervour of nationalism. Naturally Hitler could not let his mother to become sad by his rejection of fulfilling the father's wishes. But time brought a hope on behalf of his determination in the form of illness. His optimistic nature sought hope even in his illness and his illness seemed to him as his assistance. The doctor advised his mother very strongly not under any circumstances to allow him to take up a career, which would necessitate working in an office. He ordered that he should give up attendance at the Realschule for a year at least. Then the long-standing family conflict about the career came to an end. But Hitler was not destined to be happy for more time. Two years later his mother's sudden demise came as a terrible blow to him. He also lost the love of his dear mother. Like his father, to cope the miserable situation and with an indomitable resolution in his heart alongwith his uncertain future he left for Vienna. At this dilemma also he was firm to become 'something' but not a civil servant. Now he was sure not to let his determination to stagger.

Before his mother's death Hitler had come to Vienna to take the entrance exam for the Academy of Fine Arts. He was sure of his success but it was a great shock to him when his hopes of success shattered after the declaration of the result. But he realized that he was better in architectural designing and he knew that he ought to become an architect. But in this respect his fate did not favour him as to get the admission in the Technical building school; a leaving certificate from the Middle School was must which he did not have. After his mother's death when he came to Vienna he had only inspiration of his father's life and the glimpses of all the struggles of life. But he was quite sure to surmount all the obstacles. He compared his dilemma to his father's struggles, who was a poor son of a village shoemaker, Hitler was in better situation. Hitler was habitual of the struggles and adventures. He was extrovert and now we can observe that he was quite optimistic towards the struggles of life. He even sought rays of hopes in very desperate times also. As so many obstacles and difficulties were to face but they helped to his firm determination. He had positive attitude towards life and was confident to overcome all the obstacles. Rather, they increased his enthusiasm and enabled him to be tough. In very positive mood he felt the dilemma of adversity helping him in struggles of life as much as he became tough and his attitude being firm towards being triumphed. Rather he appreciated the fact that he was thus saved from the emptiness of a life of case as he was thrown into a world of misery and poverty and knew how to struggle in life to overcome. So as a philosopher he also feels Adversity as to a new mother that wants to teach him by hard situations.

Thus Hitler's childhood was so revolutionary that it changed his whole life. The visible qualities and rapid development of Hitler show a growth of a revolutionary man in future. The circumstances, which were in not favour of Hitler, he just revolted against them. These are in a sequence from childhood to his adolsance and affected his mind to ponder over and to try to get over them in his own favour.

But Mahatma Gandhi in his childhood was quite meek and submissive. If Hitler opposed which did not favour his views, Gandhi was by nature blind even to the faults of elders. Having humble nature he never opposed his elders though he did the things what his morality appealed to him. It is very common thing that if a child is taught some moral values, it undergoes steadily into the mind that becomes very difficult to get rid of and the other aspect remains beyond thinking, though the distinction between the good and bad is recognized by the time. Gandhi in his autobiography mentions an incident and tells how it was beyond him to see the fault of his teacher. Though he realized that later on, but then also had same regard for the teacher.

"There is an incident which occurred at the examination during my first year at the high school and which is worth recording. Mr. Giles, the Educational Inspector, had come on a visit of inspection. He had set-up five words to write as a spelling exercise. One of the words was 'kettle'. I had misspelt it. The teacher tried to prompt me with the point of his boot, but I would not be prompted. It was beyond me to see that he wanted me to copy the spelling from my neighbour's state, for I had thought that the teacher was there to supervise us against copying. The result was that all the boys except myself were found to have spelt every word correctly. Only I had been stupid. The teacher tried later to bring this stupidity home to me, but without effect. I never could learn the art of 'copying'.

Gandhi had a sense of right and wrong though he also accepts 'For I had learnt to carry out the orders of elders, not to scan their actions.'

Gandhi was not interested in any reading beyond his school book 'The daily lessons had to be done, because I disliked being taken to task by my teacher as much as I disliked deceiving him. Therefore I would do the lessons, but often without my mind in them? It was his sincere regards and truthfulness towards his teachers that he had to study. Though he was not interested in extra reading however he came to read a book of a play about Shravan's devotion to his parents, *i.e.*, *Sharavana Pitribhakti Nataka.*' He read it with intense interest and the story influenced him greatly. The influence of the play Harishchandra also captured his heart. He felt great enthusiasm to see it. The impression was so intense that he always asked to himself day and night 'Why should not all be truthful like Harishchandra?' That was the incident to influence greatly the mind of the child that raised him so high from the common masses. It was the preaching of the truthfulness that had great impression that under any circumstance he took a resolution to follow.

There has been a peculiar tradition of child-marriage in India and how Gandhi could be escaped from this tradition. He was married in very tender age of thirteen. Though about marriage the perception of this child was 'the prospect of good clothes to wear, drum beating, marriage processions, rich dinners and a strange girl to play with. The carnal desire came later.'

Obviously, Gandhi was unaware of the responsibilities after marriage rather he was happy to have a girl to play with. 'Little did I dream then that one day I would severely criticize my father for having married me as a child. Everything on that day seemed to me right and proper and pleasing. Though he also accepts that he took no time in assuming the authority of a husband. As he had a passion to follow the truth and his duties, he was dutiful towards his wife. The circumstances make a person, responsible. In this tender age the childhood was taken away from the child. How much he should be mature about the relation. The responsibility was entrusted to him to which he was quite immature to subsist. Though Gandhi did not consider the real meaning of a married life, but there was a sense of authority of being a husband. Rather he did not understand how to behave with a wife and what are the duties of a husband towards his wife; and he started to impose restrictions on her. That became the reason of the quarrel between them. Quite naturally, both the children being married, did not understand the true meaning of duties towards their life partners. For this also Gandhi gives the reason that his severity were all based on love. How farther the imagination of a child might go as he wanted to make his wife an ideal wife. His restrictions were imposed on her since he thought the life, the identity of his wife his own.

So the childhood of Gandhi went on with the strange plight as his studies and marriage went on hand in hand. As far as his studies is concerned he was always sincere towards his duty as there was a passion to follow the path of truth. It didn't matter where he was interested or not the consequence was that he also won the affection of his teachers. Due to his sincere studies his progress and character certificates were quite well, he even won prizes and scholarships. But he was quite sensitive and always liked to have middle path of success. He, in his autobiography introspects, "My own recollection is that I had not any high regard for my ability. I used to be astonished whenever I won prizes and scholarships. But I very jealously guarded my character. The little least blemish drew tears from my eyes. When I merited, or seemed to the teacher to merit, a rebuke, it was unbearable for me." As a child he disliked any exercise, cricket or football and gymnastics. The reason was that he was shy and he also wished to serve his father. He mentions an interesting incident how he was convicted of telling a lie as he did not do that it pained him deeply. As he could not speak a lie he could not bear to be convicted of lying. His headmaster was a disciplinarian, a man of method and a good teacher. He had made gymnastics and cricket compulsory for boys of the upper standards. But Gandhi had a keen desire to serve his father and he did not want to waste his time. He requested Mr. Gimi to exempt him, but the request was refused. His school was in morning shift and he had to go from home to the school for gymnastics at 4 O'clock in the afternoon. As he had no watch, the cloud deceived him. And before he reached the school the boys had all left. Mr. Gimi asked the reason for his absence and what Gandhi explained, he did not believe and Gandhi was to pay a fine of one or two annas. He became harassed as he could not prove his innocence. He even cried but learnt that 'a man of truth must also be a man of care.'

As Gandhi had lost one year due to his marriage, and he had been an industrious boy, he was allowed to skip a class as compensation. He was promoted to fourth standard. English being the medium of instruction and Geometry as a new subject became difficult to him. He could not follow what the teacher taught. His ambition and teacher's belief in him created a fear of the double discredit, so his efforts made the subject easy to overcome. Sanskrit also seemed difficult subject to him but the inspiration of his teacher helped him in getting through the subject.

Gandhi had been a social reformer from his school days. Many instances may be cited from his autobiography. He was warned of having a bad friend. In this regard his optimistic opinion of his philosophy keeps him in a well position of social reformer.

"I know he has weaknesses you attribute to him, but you do not know his virtues. He cannot lead me astray, as my association with him is meant to reform him. For I am sure that if he reforms his ways, he will be a splendid man. I beg you not to be anxious on my account."

Though later on Gandhi considered that in friendship there is very little scope for reform. 'All the exclusive intimacies are to be avoided' for man takes in vice far more readily than virtue. Now his view became broader, as his effort to cultivate an intimate friendship proved a failure, as an embodiment of the dream and vision, he perceived the meaning of friendship that "he who would be friends with God must remain alone, or make the whole world his friend."

During the era of Gandhi the English ruled over India. People were struggling for their freedom. There was a false notion of meat-eating in Rajkot. People had inferiority complex as the foreigners had ruled them. Gandhi came to know the notion by his friends, 'We are a weak people because we do not eat meat. The English are able to rule over us, because they are meat-eaters." Different pleas on behalf of meat-eating were represented before him by his friends. He was dazzled to see others to be stronger and himself feeble and as he also wanted to overcome his fear of thieves, ghosts and serpents of which he used to be haunted. The desire of eating meat was aroused in him. A bad deed gets its way easier. But Gandhi became on its behalf as to overcome the English. Though there was abhorrence of meat-eating in his family but he persuaded himself that 'mere hiding the deed from parents was no departure from truth.' His meat-eating along with his one brother and friend went on for about a year. But unconsciously he had a disgust for this deed and as a consequence he was haunted by a horrible nightmare. He also felt shame of hiding the truth like a thief from his parents. Often after these surreptitious feasts he had to lie before his mother when she asked about dinner at home. All these facts tormented him and he came to the opinion 'deceiving and lying to one's father and mother is worse than not eating meat.' Though Gandhi was aware that he was in a bad company of the friend but he did not abjure that company. He was in favour of charity towards uncharitable. But his zeal for reforming his friend proved disastrous for him. These experiences and experiments to indulge in bad deeds and then to reform himself and others made him strong in following his resolution of truth. He was also indulged in other bad deeds which, while engrossed tormented him but he overcome all these. He became addicted to smoking, and the first deed of theft was committed when he was twelve or thirteen and the second when he was of fifteen. But he resolved never to steal again. He was not afraid of being beaten by his father if he confessed, he was afraid of the pain to cause to his father. He wrote a confession and submitted to his father and asked his forgiveness. But unexpectedly his father's pearl-drops of love which trickled down his cheeks washed his sin. At this age of fifteen he learnt an object-lesson in Ahimsa. It was pure Ahimsa, which purifies the soul. There is no limit to its power. His confession was of the purest type of repentance.

Gandhi, in this way learnt through the experiences of life. Like the two faces of a coin, he experienced both the positive and negative aspects of life. However, he always remained adhered to his resolution of truth and non-violence. He came to follow these two doctrines as these were the true experiences and along with them he always had felt having a serene life.

To conclude, the lives of these two great leaders arouse great interest in reader to go through. Their childhood have proved that coming events cast their shadows before. Their traits of adherence to their resolutions proved them to become the staunch follower of their dogmas. However, the paths were diagonally opposite to each other. As a result of their resolutions they stood at the top of the leaders of the world. Hitler, having great passion for nationalism and firm resolution, became vehement dictator as he suffered a lot in his life from early childhood. He considered the policies of getting his position and reaching his goal from very young age. He never gave in his mission and the result is before the world. Whereas Gandhi went on living his life facing the problems by the path of Ahimsa as he considered it the path of spiritualism and purification of soul. He was never weary of doing good, and proved that pure gold does not fear the flame.

References

Gandhi, M.K., 1923. *My Experiments with Truth*. Ahmedabad: Sarvodaya. Reprint 1990.

Hitler, Adolf. 1940. *Mein Kampf*. Bonn.

Contributors

Basavaraj Naikar, Professor and Chairperson, Department of English, Dharvad University, Karnataka.

Mary Conde, Professor, School of English and Drama, Queen Mary, University of London, England.

Shubha Tiwari, Head, Department of English, APS University, Rewa, Madhya Pradesh.

B. Parvathi, Associate Professor, Department of English, Andhra University, Visakhapatnam, Andhra Pradesh.

Madhu Singh, Lecturer, Department of English and European Languages, Lucknow University, Lucknow, Uttar Pradesh.

Alka Saxena, Reader, Department of English, DAV College, Kanpur, Uttar Pradesh.

Sharada Iyer, Head, Department of English, Vasanta College, Rajghat, Varanasi, Uttar Pradesh.

Purnima Mehta, Professor and Head, Department of English, Bhavnagar University, Gujarat.

Sadhana Agrawal, Assistant Professor, English, Maharajah College, Chhatarpur, Madhya Pradesh.

Marina Goglio, Research Scholar, Department of Oriental Studies, University of Turin, Italy.

Esterino Adami, Research Associate, Department of Oriental Studies, University of Turin, Italy.

Shubha Dwivedi, M.Phil. Student, University of Delhi, New Delhi.

Awadhesh K. Mishra, Research Scholar, APS University, Rewa, Madhya Pradesh.

Neha Nigam, PG Student, APS University, Rewa, Madhya Pradesh.

Kiran Shukla, Rearch Scholar, A.P.S.U. Rewa, Madhya Pradesh.